FROM CRISIS
TO CALLING

FROM CRISIS TO CALLING

Finding Your Moral Center in the Toughest Decisions

Sasha Chanoff
and
David Chanoff

BK°

Berrett–Koehler Publishers, Inc.
a BK Currents book

Berrett-Koehler Publishers, Inc.
1333 Broadway, Suite 1000, Oakland, CA 94612-1921
Tel: (510) 817-2277   Fax: (510) 817-2278   www.bkconnection.com

Ordering Information

Quantity Sales. Special discounts are available on quantity purchases by corporations, associations, and others. For details, contact the "Special Sales Department" at the Berrett-Koehler address above.

Individual Sales. Berrett-Koehler publications are available through most bookstores. They can also be ordered directly from Berrett-Koehler: Tel: (800) 929-2929; Fax: (802) 864-7626; www.bkconnection.com

Orders for College Textbook/Course Adoption Use. Please contact Berrett-Koehler: Tel: (800) 929-2929; Fax: (802) 864-7626.

Orders by U.S. Trade Bookstores and Wholesalers. Please contact Ingram Publisher Services, Tel: (800) 509-4887; Fax: (800) 838-1149; E-mail: customer .service@ ingrampublisherservices.com; or visit www.ingrampublisherservices .com/Ordering for details about electronic ordering.

Berrett-Koehler and the BK logo are registered trademarks of Berrett-Koehler Publishers, Inc.

Printed in the United States of America

Berrett-Koehler books are printed on long-lasting acid-free paper. When it is available, we choose paper that has been manufactured by environmentally responsible processes. These may include using trees grown in sustainable forests, incorporating recycled paper, minimizing chlorine in bleaching, or recycling the energy produced at the paper mill.

Library of Congress Cataloging-in-Publication Data

Names: Chanoff, Sasha, author. | Chanoff, David, author.
Title: From crisis to calling : finding your moral center in the toughest decisions / Sasha Chanoff and David Chanoff.
Description: First edition. | Oakland, CA : Berrett-Koehler Publishers, Inc., [2016]
Identifiers: LCCN 2015050641 | ISBN 9781626564497 (pbk.)
Subjects: LCSH: Leadership--Moral and ethical aspects--Case studies. | Refugees--Africa--Case studies. | Crisis management--Moral and ethical aspects--Case studies. | Decision making--Moral and ethical aspects--Case studies.
Classification: LCC HM1261 .C444 2016 | DDC 303.3/4--dc23
LC record available at http://lccn.loc.gov/2015050641

First Edition

21 20 19 18 17 16   10 9 8 7 6 5 4 3 2 1

Interior design: Laura Lind Design   *Edit:* Lunaea Weatherstone
Cover design: Leslie Walzer/Crowfoot Design   *Proofread:* Karen Hill Green
Production service: Linda Jupiter Productions   *Index:* Paula C. Durbin-Westby

This book is dedicated to all those who have lost their lives in the Congo, and to David Derthick and Sheikha Ali, my heroes.

Sasha Chanoff

To my wife, Lissu. We have shared everything meaningful in our lives together—this too.

David Chanoff

CONTENTS

FOREWORD

Throughout history, leaders have experienced "crucible moments"—times when they are suddenly thrust into the middle of a crisis and must quickly gather their wits, sort out right from wrong, and act decisively. Those moments often shape them for the rest of their lives. In the case of the best leaders, those tests also become the making of their moral centers.

Think of a young Gandhi early in the 20th century, beginning his life as a barrister in a foreign land, South Africa. The moment when a conductor threw him off a train because he was Indian was not only a humiliation, it was a crucible that propelled him to become a protest leader and eventually win independence for his native people.

Think of the personal dilemma Eleanor Roosevelt had in 1918 as her husband Franklin returned home with pneumonia from a trans-Atlantic voyage. She had to help him with his luggage and in opening his trunk discovered a packet of love letters exchanged with Eleanor's social secretary. A mother of six and a strong believer that her husband would be a great American leader, Eleanor had to decide quickly whether to leave or stay in her marriage. She stayed and helped him become president. But more than that, she began to devote herself to service outside the home, and she became a towering figure in securing human rights in America and the world beyond.

Or think of two very different men at mid-century: one a young Martin Luther King Jr., taking up his pastorate in Birmingham, being thrust into racial conflict when whites threw Rosa Parks off a public bus. King went to his pulpit to urge his parishioners to protest but soon saw that despite his contrary inclinations, he must go to the streets, too. His protests brought a civil rights revolution. Not

long thereafter, a man who was sometimes King's opponent, Bobby
Kennedy, went to Mississippi and discovered hunger and discrimina-
tion that horrified him. He became an immensely important voice for
social justice.

Crucibles are moments that can change lives and change history.
And so they have in the case of Sasha Chanoff and his dad, David.
Early in the pages of this stirring book, they tell the story of Sasha's
own crucible in the heart of Africa. There he faced, for the first time,
life-and-death decisions about how to respond to a refugee crisis.
And there, from that moment, Sasha discovered his own moral values and how they transformed him into the world-class leader he has
become today.

These crisis situations, the authors tell us, often go much further
than simply putting people in touch with the values they need in order to become authentic leaders. "Dilemmas," they write, "require
decisions; decisions require actions. Sometimes the required actions
reach deep. They generate a full investment of the self—that is to say,
they constitute a calling. When that happens, it not only opens us
up to *who* we are but to *what* we are." In other words, crises have the
power to reveal qualities we harbor within ourselves that may have
previously gone unrecognized. They can clarify our sense of ourselves
and our capabilities.

After his Congo experience, Sasha founded RefugePoint, an
NGO that works throughout Africa to find solutions for individuals and communities in imminent danger. They acted not a moment
too soon. The world is now experiencing its biggest refugee crisis in
recorded history: more than 60 million people are now displaced by
conflict across the globe. The migrant crisis could destabilize Western
Europe, and it is causing enormous human suffering in other conti-
nents such as Africa.

RefugePoint has become one of the most successful organizations in the world in addressing this catastrophe. Over the past decade, it has successfully helped more than 32,454 refugees gain access to resettlement. It has also become a role model for countless others. In 2013, on behalf of the Gleitsman Foundation, I was proud to present to Sasha the prestigious Gleitsman International Activist Award, bestowed every other year by a global selection committee representing the Center for Public Leadership at the Harvard Kennedy School. Students and faculty alike were enthralled by Sasha's story and by the lessons he brought to his leadership.

Happily, Sasha and his dad have now turned his experiences and lessons learned into this important book about moral leadership, *From Crisis to Calling*. It is a work that has application far beyond the refugee world: leaders of NGOs, corporate leaders, and leaders of public institutions face crucible moments, too—times when they face dilemmas, must choose between right and wrong, and then act decisively. Unfortunately, the leaders who make the right moral choices can stay anonymous and unrecognized. But the dozens of scandals we see in business, politics, and even in the nonprofit world remind us that these dilemmas are constant, and indeed, the seductions that lead to moral failure are always present, always beckoning. Crucibles cannot be avoided. The question the Chanoffs address is: how can we best prepare for them before they arrive?

The Chanoffs trace a five-step pathway that starts with being prepared and opening your eyes, then moves to confronting yourself, knowing yourself, and taking courage. Importantly, they teach these lessons through stories that are gripping in their drama and power. From two prominent CEOs, the emergency director of an international NGO, and a former US surgeon general to a distinguished business professor, a family physician, and a former Navy SEAL,

Sasha and David bring together the journeys of individuals from all walks of life.

From Crisis to Calling serves several purposes. It acquaints readers with stories about the meaningful role moral values play in decision making and leadership. It explains ways we can reveal the inner qualities that we all share yet not all of us find. And it prepares us to take the steps that may well help us fulfill our potential as leaders.

From Crisis to Calling is also an antidote of sorts. While the public failings of leaders cover the front pages of newspapers and lead the nightly news, Sasha and David bring us the stories of unsung leaders who have faced tough decisions with morality and grace. They remind us that empathy and compassion—altruism—are deeply rooted in us. That they are there to be nurtured. Novelist Graham Greene once wrote of "those interior courts where our true decisions are made." The Chanoffs, father and son, dive deep into our interior courts, looking for, and finding, the inner qualities that define the truly great and good leaders among us.

David Gergen
February 2016

PREFACE

This is a very personal book for both me and my father and co-author, David Chanoff. Its origins are in a seminal experience I had as a young refugee worker in Africa. Early in the year 2000, a colleague and I were sent into the Democratic Republic of the Congo on a rescue mission to evacuate survivors of countrywide massacres. I did not anticipate that the experience would shape and change me as it did. But the unexpected life-and-death dilemma that confronted us there in a country torn apart by war has forced on me years of reflection. During that mission we faced a decision about whom to take with us, if we could, and whom to leave behind, if we had to. I've pondered ever since: Did we do the right thing? What if we had lost more people? Could I have lived with myself if everyone had perished?

My colleague and I argued our options out during a long, sleepless night, the two of us on different sides about what to do. I had never before been tested by anything remotely resembling this. It was, for both of us, what one writer on moral decision making calls "a crucible," the kind of experience that has the potential to transform a person from who he or she was into somebody with a far clearer sense of self and the rock-bottom values that matter most.

I was unprepared to make a decision of this kind. I had only been working in Africa for six months then. I had never worked in a country at war. I had never had to hire armed guards to protect massacre survivors in a place where many of their family members and friends had been hunted down and killed. I had never had to deal with violent, duplicitous government officials out to either use our rescue operation for their own purposes or shut it down and do their worst to the people we were trying to protect.

During the mission I took precautions to make sure the Congolese officials did not know our precise evacuation plans. Government spies had likely bugged my room and were monitoring emails and phone calls. In spite of this I felt the need to communicate with my parents, to let them know I was all right and to give them some idea about what was happening. Just as I had never done this sort of thing, I knew that this was a new experience for them as parents, worrying about a child of theirs working in a place of great danger.

With a Finnish mom and an American dad, I grew up bilingual. Even if my emails were monitored, I thought it unlikely that the spies could decipher Finnish. So in brief moments at the computer I fired off emails to my parents in my mom's native language, telling them I was okay and a little about what was going on.

After the rescue operation my dad, David, and I started up a conversation that has gone on for years about what happened back then: how that life-and-death dilemma changed the person I was, and how hard-choice dilemmas have impacted others we knew. For myself, that experience shaped the way I looked at people who had suffered violence and persecution in their home countries that forced them into lives as refugees. Eventually I founded a non-governmental organization (NGO), RefugePoint, whose mission is to protect the lives of those who are overlooked or forgotten by the world's humanitarian networks.

Over the last ten years as I've built this organization, I've continually returned to that decision point in the Congo. It has become a guidepost for my leadership because it forced me to think about my own values and the best way to express those through my actions.

As RefugePoint grew, the talks with my dad increasingly focused on to how to build and lead an organization. Eventually those talks extended to discussions with our Berrett-Koehler editor about my particular experience and how that related to leadership more broadly.

My interest in understanding what this decision meant for me grew into an exploration of what critical decision points have meant for others, and about the nature of leadership, and into this book.

And who better to co-write it with than my dad? He was intimately engaged from those first emails he received from the Congo, and he has been a colleague as well in the evolution of RefugePoint. Not least, in his own career he has collaborated on books with leaders in the military, business, health, politics, and other fields, many of whom have experienced their own critical decision points.

The book is in two parts. In Part I, I tell the story of the Congo rescue operation in my own voice and in some detail. We regard this as a kind of "story of stories," the platform for our thoughts about how people make moral decisions and how those experiences can shape who we are and how we interact with our own organizations and communities. In Part II, my dad and I go on to tell the stories of people from many walks of life who have themselves faced decision points that have been pivotal for them. These stories speak to our common need to know who we are. They tell us how this essential knowledge of our own values can transform the impact we make on those around us, how it can, and often does, lead to a calling that we may well have had no idea we harbored within ourselves.

From Crisis to Calling is about moral leadership, the kind that doesn't leave anyone behind. It's about how to identify this kind of leadership within yourself by using crucible moments, or decision points, to hone in on and bring out the humanitarian values such as empathy and compassion that are intrinsic in all of us. It's about how to take advantage of the hardest decisions in our lives in order to tune in to our moral core and use it as a lodestar for leadership.

Sasha Chanoff

THE FIVE-STEP PATHWAY TO MORAL DECISION MAKING

*We found that every leader in our study, young
or old, had undergone at least one intense,
transformational experience.*
Warren Bennis

In the middle of difficulty lies opportunity.
John Archibald Wheeler

Today a growing wealth of research supports the idea that leadership that is moral, other-centered, trustworthy, and compassionate empowers success. Social scientists such as Dacher Keltner, Martin Seligman, and Barbara Fredrickson have shown that the capacity for altruism is critical to good leadership. "Leaders, in every field," says business guru Warren Bennis, "are richly endowed with empathy." "The crucial decision," says distinguished Harvard business professor Joseph Badaracco, "is not *whether* we should rely on our ethical intuitions, but *how* to do so."

From Crisis to Calling holds these insights as truths essential to true leadership and, more importantly, critical to the business of living a good, fulfilling life, a life that affords a true sense of pride.

Some of our most prominent thinkers about leadership have reached similar conclusions about how character is formed. In searching out the essentials of how leaders are made, they have spent years observing and talking with famous and not so famous leaders about their lives. What have they found?

In his seminal book *On Becoming a Leader*, Warren Bennis wrote that leadership "always emerged after some rite of passage, often a stressful one." In a follow-up study, *Geeks and Geezers*, he elaborated: "We found that every leader in our study, young or old, had undergone at least one intense, transformational experience. That transformational experience was at the very heart of becoming a leader. The descriptive term we found ourselves using is *crucible*." Bill George wrote in his equally influential *True North: Discover Your Authentic Leadership*, "It is under pressure—when your success, your career, or your life hangs in the balance—that you must decide what your values are. When you are forced to make trade-offs between your values under difficult circumstances, you learn what is most important in your life and what you are prepared to sacrifice for."

Joseph Badaracco focused his discussion in *Defining Moments* more narrowly. The true test, he argues, comes when people must decide between two courses that may both be right. These "right-versus-right choices are best understood as *defining moments* . . . they reveal, they test, and they shape. In other words, a right-versus-right decision can reveal a manager's basic values . . . It shapes the character of the person and, in some cases, the organization."

Crucibles for Bennis. *Defining moments* for Badaracco. *Finding your true north* for George. Each of these writers looks at life and leadership from the standpoint of moral transformation and the discovery of an essential self—the fundamental values that define you as a person. Each in his own way makes the point that this essential self is essential also to the organizations the leader is part of. Leaders imbue their organizations and communities with values—that is, with the values they find within themselves. Authentic leaders are those for whom the values they live in their personal lives are the same as those they live in their professional lives.

Leadership writers, no matter how famous, tend to be known mainly within the business world, a vast yet limited sphere. But practitioners such as Bennis, Badaracco, and George—and perhaps Peter Drucker most of all—teach us universal lessons about human psychology, true for those of us in other fields of endeavor and true for those of us who live our lives in quieter, more inconspicuous ways. Business is, after all, a great moral theater, driven by the profit motive yet bound by commonly accepted ethical values. These values are often imposed by law, but they also invoke the better angels of our nature. Business is a stage where the desire to act for advantage often plays starkly against our more moral selves whose call we hear, if sometimes only faintly, amidst the competing noises of our lives.

Consequently, the "business" books leading thinkers write are often far more than business books. They suggest that business is a key to the human enterprise generally—the "business" of how we live our lives and how we should live our lives. True, then, for all of us.

It's one thing to say that character is formed, or discovered, in crucibles or defining moments. But ordinarily we do not look to get ourselves into situations like that. If anything, our default is to stay away from them, from the stress they bring, the failure they threaten, the difficult life changes they may portend. We are more motivated to stay in our safety zones, the places we feel comfortable. Others have expectations of us based on what we've done before and what they think we should be doing now. Those are forceful expectations. We know the behaviors that have worked for us in the past; we have little incentive and little desire to change those. We don't want to push the envelopes we've woven around ourselves. Whether they're constricting or spacious, we've woven them for a reason.

Yet none of us can avoid facing critical decisions. They come with the human territory. We may need to fire a subordinate or perhaps lay off an entire group. We need to choose between alternatives that may inflict pain on a friend or a family member. We face such decisions inevitably. When we do, we can choose to just forge ahead, turning a blind eye to the human side of what we think needs to be done. We can rationalize the necessity of our decision. We can compartmentalize—this is what I had to do, but it doesn't affect the person I really am. We can disregard the moral dimension of the decision, because that is easiest for us; it allows us to get on with our work and our lives.

But the truth is that such rationales—apparent necessity, the expectations of others, fear of failure—can never bring meaningful growth or change. Taking the easy or expected route may provide some transient gain, but far more often those kinds of responses leave us stranded in the same rut. As one business writer put it, "If you do the same as you've always done, you'll get the same as you've always gotten." Critical decisions carry with them the opportunity for transformation and creative growth, but only if we understand them that way. Only if we embrace them for their potential as turning points for ourselves and consequently for those whom we lead and whose lives we impact.

From Crisis to Calling reveals the opportunities present in the hardest decisions and explains how to take advantage of crises and make the unrecognized power of altruism work for you. It sets out the five principles inherent in confronting critical decisions:

1. Be prepared.

2. Open your eyes.

3. Confront yourself.

4. Know yourself.

5. Take courage.

Through moving stories of leaders from business, the military, humanitarian agencies, health care, and other fields, we will see these principles come alive in ways that illuminate and instruct. Readers will learn how others have built or changed their organizations and their own lives in response to the hardest challenges of their careers by opening themselves up to this five-step critical decision process. *From Crisis to Calling* shows how such challenges so often transform the nature of leadership and create different, more ethical, and more productive leadership practices.

From Crisis to Calling is in two parts. Part I is the story of Sasha and his colleague and the critical decision they faced. We tell the story in its entirety, then look at how it embodies the five-step critical decision process. Part II describes dramatic experiences in the lives of others that illuminate one or more of these steps.

Our goal is to engage leaders in business, nonprofit, and other fields, along with the general reading public, in this "hard decision" phenomenon. There is a transformative potential in choices where options are limited, painful, and full of the possibility of failure. Such choices may open an avenue to new, ethically centered thinking. We want readers to recognize, embrace, and act on their instinctive moral convictions, which these situations can reveal as perhaps nothing else can.

THE FIVE PRINCIPLES

1. Be Prepared.

Awareness is the first requirement. Situations arise that have a moral stake at their core. Be aware that these are decision points that can fundamentally affect the direction of your life and the life of your organization. Often we are closed to the possibilities inherent in such situations. We veer automatically toward the known, the conventional, the safe. We lean toward what others may expect of us and what we may expect of ourselves. We all too easily look the other way when a hard situation confronts us, particularly if opening our eyes might take us out of our comfort zone and down a risky path. Being prepared primes you to recognize these situations for the potential they afford.

2. Open Your Eyes.

Being prepared allows you to open your eyes to examine the decision confronting you with candor. You have given yourself permission to leave your cubicle and accept the possibility that the expected path, the conventional path, is not the only path, and, in fact, may well be the wrong path. Now at least you can see the issue clearly, in particular the moral options facing you.

3. Confront Yourself.

Once you have opened your eyes to the challenge in front of you, you need to explore what to do. Often these decisions are not clear-cut. It's easy to understand a decision when we are presented with a clear right and a clear wrong. It's harder to uncover the proper course forward when any action can bring about good as well as bad consequences—which is often the case in complex organizational decisions. It's important, then, to explore and discuss, to have someone who can challenge your beliefs and values. Great literature is full of iconic helmsmen who are able to lead the hero through the labyrinths of doubt. You may have some wise counselor or partner of this kind; if not, you will need to be your own helmsman. Either way, be aware that you need the argument, you need to undergo the hard test. Otherwise, opening your eyes may not be enough.

4. Know Yourself.

The process of confrontation and discussion will clarify the decision you have to make, but it will likely have more profound consequences as well. The values you have brought with you to this crucial decision may have served you decently to this point in your career. But facing a moral crux—accepting it, opening your eyes to it, confronting yourself over it—can reveal the underpinnings of your own moral life that may have been opaque to you or perhaps relegated to the sidelines or suppressed in the course of building your career. Moral crucibles have great power to create change. They can put you in touch with your inner self and connect you with your past experiences and even your family history in a way ordinary life does not. They can highlight for you the gap between who you are and who you would like to be. They can give you the wherewithal to tap into the underlying empathy, compassion, and feeling for others so significant in living a fulfilling life and creating an organizational culture that embodies its leader's principal values.

5. Take Courage.

Once you have tapped into your own set of primary values, you will likely understand what the right course of action is for you. That course of action may be the more difficult one. It may bring with it the risk of failure and many negative consequences. How do you make the right decision in the face of fear and potential obstacles? Courage is the crucial quality here, which is always magnified by the force of moral conviction.

Sasha's story takes place in the humanitarian sphere, but the Congo rescue mission story is a paradigm for decision making in many fields. Business leaders frequently confront situations that call for difficult moral judgments, pitting financial pressures against moral considerations. We see their failures regularly, from Enron, WorldCom, and Volkswagen to others that make the news from week to week. Even in the normal course of business life, when businesses are operating within the expected norms, the conventional response to such moral decision points is to make the apparently more profitable choice.

For managers—especially in business but in other fields as well—the concept of moral leadership may feel idealistic, abstract, something we'd like to practice but that seems distant from the real world of efficiencies, productivity, and the bottom line. Leadership often assumes the ability to make tough-minded decisions that subordinate feelings of altruism, sympathy, and compassion to the need for results. By this criterion, leaders need to be hard-nosed realists, maybe not impervious to human feeling, but able to rise above it in order to achieve success for themselves in their careers and success for their organizations in their businesses.

That commonplace wisdom—the leader as a realist able and willing to apply cool, impersonal reasoning to what are often messy and painful human problems—seems natural, an inbuilt requirement for successful managers. "The boss is a bastard" is a cliché. The boss may or may not be a bastard, but he or she must have a well-developed impersonal and hard-edged approach to making decisions.

A look below the surface reveals another side of leadership.

The *Fortune* 100 Best Companies to Work For operate on a variety of business models. They provide different pay levels and perks for their employees, but their cultures are universally built on trust, fairness, equitability, and ethical leadership. They are typically philanthropic; they give back to their communities. They incorporate a core set of values that are often at odds with conventional bottom-line thinking. They endow their employees with a sense of dignity, potential, and self-worth. They do this, as Warren Bennis and others argue, first and foremost because their leaders embody empathic, humane values that flow down like water to those around them. Such individuals are, in Daniel Goleman's phrase, "primal leaders." They "resonate." Bill George calls them "authentic leaders," true to themselves.

Many of these leaders have eye-opening defining moments when convention and commonplace wisdom seem to dictate a course of action, but a challenging dilemma reveals a different path, marked by empathy and compassion.

This "hard decision" experience is rarely explored, yet it is a widespread phenomenon in moral development that has great relevance for understanding leadership and institutions. It illuminates the path leaders should be explicitly aware of—that these kinds of decisions can and do serve as guides through the intersection of personal values and institutional or organizational leadership.

This is the subject *From Crisis to Calling* will take up. We will be looking at individuals whose experiences illustrate the different dimensions of our paradigm. We will look at the situations that motivated them and at the consequences for their lives and the lives of their organizations. The ultimate message is about how challenging situations can reveal deep personal values and about the power and fulfillment that come from investing your work with compassion, empathy, and the awareness of others.

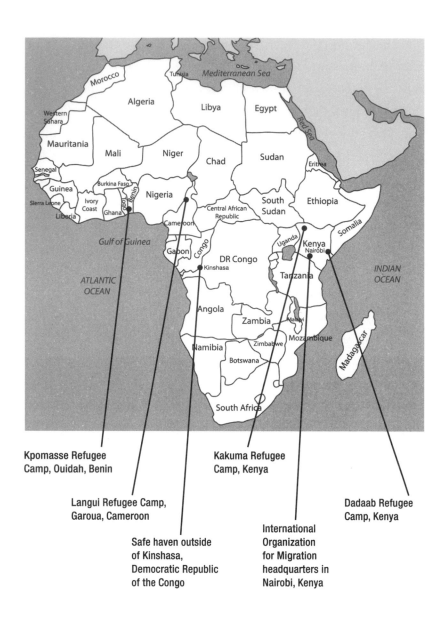

Kpomasse Refugee
Camp, Ouidah, Benin

Langui Refugee Camp,
Garoua, Cameroon

Kakuma Refugee
Camp, Kenya

Safe haven outside
of Kinshasa,
Democratic Republic
of the Congo

International
Organization
for Migration
headquarters in
Nairobi, Kenya

Dadaab Refugee
Camp, Kenya

PART I

THE CONGO
RESCUE
MISSION

SASHA CHANOFF WAS A YOUNG FIELD OFFICER FOR THE INTERNATIONAL Organization for Migration recently arrived in Africa when he and a colleague, Sheikha Ali, were sent into the Congo on a life-and-death rescue mission. The Congo was aflame with violence. In response to events that followed the Rwandan genocide, Congo's strongman government had launched a campaign to eradicate the country's Tutsi minority. Many villages had been attacked. Thousands had been killed, many in atrocious ways. Amidst the waves of anti-Tutsi terror, the Clinton administration, together with a number of other governments and international humanitarian agencies, had pressured the Congolese regime into setting up a protected compound outside Kinshasa. Tutsis who could find their way there would be evacuated to UN camps in Benin and Cameroon; from there, they could be resettled in the United States after the required interviews and security checks.

The International Organization for Migration (IOM) had managed three evacuations from the Congo before the process broke down under the weight of violence, intimidation, and corruption. The Congolese had arbitrarily kept back 112 Tutsi men, women, and children from the final evacuation. With the end of the evacuations, these 112 had been left in the compound to die.

Continued pressure, though, forced the Congolese to allow one final mission to extricate those who had been left behind. Sasha and Sheikha Ali were sent in to carry out the operation. They were under strict orders to take the 112 people on their list and no others. Attempting to include anyone other than those for whom they had permission would almost certainly abort the mission and result in the deaths of the 112.

When Sasha and Sheikha arrived at the compound, they found that the International Committee for the Red Cross (ICRC) had brought in thirty-two widows and orphans the previous day, rescued from an execution center where they had been starved and brutalized for sixteen months. The women and children looked like World War II concentration camp victims. Without nutrition and medical help they were unlikely to survive more than a few days. Sasha and Sheikha had to decide what to do. Should they take those on the approved list and leave the widows and orphans to their fate? Or should they attempt to include them and risk everyone's lives?

ONE

BE PREPARED

Confronting the Unexpected Dilemma

Sasha's story begins here, on his and Sheikha's first day in the Congo. They had been to the US embassy and to the Congolese so-called Ministry of Human Rights, which was anything but. At the day's end they met with representatives of the International Committee for the Red Cross, the United Nations Refugee Agency, and with officials from other nations supporting the Tutsi rescue operation—the "contact group." They made it clear they would only be taking the 112 people on the list and no one else. Sasha begins by describing what happened then.

I was just finishing my briefing when the man from the International Committee for the Red Cross stood up. "I understand what you said." His voice had an edge to it. "You're only going to take the people on your list. You say you don't have permission for anyone else and you say you don't have any extra seats on the plane. But now there's a new group of people you have to take. Yesterday we brought thirty-two widows and orphans into the protection center from one of the ex-ecution prisons. They were there for sixteen months. All the adult males were killed. None of these women and children will last another week. You must put them on this flight."

David Derthick, our boss, had warned me about the contact group players. "They're all going to have people they'll want you to take out," he said. "They'll pressure you to do it. Don't take them! Just go in, tell them what the plan is and stop there. If you let anyone outside the list on that plane, you'll kill the whole mission. The Congolese will flood you with fraudulent cases and you won't have any way of saying no. The whole thing will implode and you'll lose everybody. They'll kill everyone who's left. You tell them. Just the list. No one else."

The ICRC man was still standing. "Unfortunately," I told him, "the flight is completely full. We don't have any more room on the plane. We simply are not able to take further cases. The list is closed. This evacuation is closed." But as I spoke, my eyes met Sheikha's. Widows and orphans, right out of a death camp. We never expected anything like this. What were we supposed to do now?

At seven the next morning, a beat-up black compact was waiting at the curb outside our hotel. Sheikha knew the driver, a short, fat man with a furtive look. He had worked for Sheikha and David during the earlier evacuations. We had also hired three other drivers to be on call for Immigration Department or Ministry of Human Rights officials we might need to ferry around for one reason or another. On the previous missions, if David or Sheikha needed an official's presence or documents delivered, or if there was an offsite meeting, people often claimed they didn't have cars—or if they did, the cars had no gas or had broken down. A money present would fix any of that, but the delays had made life difficult. We figured that if we hired cars we'd have fewer problems.

The protection center was an hour's drive from downtown Kinshasa. We drove through a sleepy suburban area that looked upscale, with nice houses and gated yards. Kinshasa itself was so tense it felt like it might explode at any moment. But the neighborhoods out here seemed peaceful. A few people were leisurely strolling on the streets, small shops were opening, the owners setting up display stands for their goods.

We pulled off the main road onto a street bordered by walled compounds. In front of us were massive black double doors set in a high wall topped by jagged glass shards jutting into the air. Sheikha gave a little nod. "This is it, the protection center." Guards with AK-47s stopped us. One of them peered into the car, then swung the doors open, and we drove through.

The walls surrounded an area that looked to be about two acres. A large gray building sat in the middle with tents set up around it. A lot of people were milling around, more than I expected. Many more than the 112 on our list. They were watching us; a car with visitors meant something. As we drove slowly toward the building, faces appeared at the car windows, staring in. Then somebody shouted, "Sheikha!"

It was as if an electric shock swept through the compound. People were suddenly streaming toward us, and in moments the car was surrounded. People were shouting, "Sheikha! Sheikha!" which quickly turned into a chant: "Sheikha Sheikha Sheikha Sheikha!" They were jostling the car, faces pressed close to get a look. I tried to keep my head down. I wanted to make myself as inconspicuous as possible, which was a crazy thought. With only Sheikha and me in the back seat, I was drawing as many stares as she was.

Before we left, David had told me that people would be overwhelmed when they saw us. "They'll be so happy to see you, they'll be crying," he said. "They won't be able to control themselves. It's going to be rough, so you better prepare yourself. Most of them are sure they're going to die there."

I thought I was prepared, but not for this mob of deliriously excited people. Sheikha had spent many months in this center, interviewing and screening people for the earlier evacuations. Many knew her from then, and those who didn't seemed to have instantly understood who she was and what she must be here for. Sheikha's arrival was the absolute best news they could possibly have. No one in the compound knew that another evacuation was planned. As far as they could tell, they were in limbo, expecting sooner or later to die—probably sooner—and sure they would never see their loved ones again. But suddenly, here was Sheikha, their hope. A straw they could grasp on to. Sheikha meant another evacuation flight must be happening. Sheikha had come back to save them.

Most of these people weren't going anywhere, though they didn't know it yet. They were going to find out soon enough: as soon as we registered the 112 and not them. Then what? When we drove in, I had seen police around, but only a few. Nowhere near enough to control this big a crowd. How this might work out was anybody's guess.

The car stopped. We were surrounded by chanting people and couldn't move. We managed to shove the doors open and get out as a couple of police tried to clear a little space. People seemed almost out of their minds to see Sheikha. They were smiling, laughing, shaking her hands, reaching out to pat her on the shoulder, trying to hug her. And Sheikha was smiling back, recognizing them, saying hello, as if she was genuinely happy to be back here.

We had to find a relatively private place where we could bring people in one at a time, or one family at a time, to interview them, record their information, and take their pictures. There were a couple of tables set up on a hill nearby, and we waded through the crowd in that direction. After climbing a few feet, I turned back around and scanned the faces, wondering if I could somehow spot the thirty-two women and orphans. Nobody stood out, except for a tall man in a fedora and sunglasses who was keeping off to one side. Unlike everyone else, he didn't seem excited or happy about Sheikha's arrival. He just stood there and watched, looking out of place and vaguely sinister. He seemed to be watching me as well as Sheikha. I wanted to say something to her, but people were still pressing around. Across the compound the guards were swinging the big doors closed and barring them. I turned away and headed up the little hill.

At the top, an ICRC person introduced himself. The International Committee for the Red Cross was in charge here. They were running the protection center, though they seemed to have only a few people. A couple of Congolese men in suits were sitting at the tables already, obviously officials, I assumed from the Ministry of Human Rights, which, given their history of corruption and abuse, was a name right out of George Orwell. I wasn't clear on what they were doing here, but Sheikha hardly took notice of them so I didn't either. Looking down at the crowd at the bottom of the hill, it seemed to me like four or five hundred people. By now they had quieted down. I took the list out of my bag and read the first names: a group of three, apparently single women as there was no notation of families. I asked one of the guards to find them and bring them up.

While we were waiting, I asked Sheikha where she thought the widows and orphans might be. Sheikha glanced over at the suits and gave me a quick look that said shut up. I kicked myself for being a little slow. These were our so-called helpers from the ministry, but they were really our minders.

The guard brought the three women to our table. I wondered what they had been through and why they were alone. What had happened to their families? But we didn't have time to start asking people about their experiences. This was Sunday. Our chartered jet was coming on Thursday. We were going to have to get the basics quickly. Name, date of birth, gender, relatives in the center. Our list had only minimal information, but from my experience in similar situations I knew that when you start asking people questions you often find that even your basic information isn't only incomplete, it's wrong.

We verified the first three and I took their pictures. Next was a family of six: mother, father, four children, including an infant. The parents looked nervous and surprisingly healthy. Again I wondered.

After them came two men, a father and son. Our list said they had been split off from the rest of their family during the last evacuation. Before Sheikha could ask the first question, the father started questioning her. Did she know how his wife was doing in Cameroon, where the evacuees had been sent? What about his three daughters? Security had grabbed him and his son from the line as they were waiting to board the plane. Why had they done that? His wife had tried to hold on to him, his daughters were hysterical. The soldiers had torn them apart. All this just came flowing out. What had happened to his family? Did they know he and his son were alive? They probably thought they were kept back to be killed. Was there any way he could get a message to them to tell them they were okay?

He was talking so fast he was practically incoherent. Sheikha told him that we couldn't get his wife a message now, but that he'd be seeing her and his daughters soon. Right now we had a lot of work to do and she needed to ask him some questions. The faster we could do that, the faster everything would go. She looked him in the eyes as she said this, and there was something about her that calmed him down. Her look said: Don't worry. We're going to get you out of here and reunited. Everything's under control. You're going to be fine.

The man took a deep breath and composed himself. Then he answered her questions. When I took him and his son aside for their photos, he said under his breath, "Please hurry. This is a dangerous place."

As we called up more individuals and families for verification, I could feel the mood shifting in the crowd below. People were supposed to stay at the bottom of the hill, but some we hadn't called found their way up to ask if they could be included. If not, when was the next flight going to be? Could we register them for that one? We didn't say anything. Not about this flight or any other flights. If their names were on the list we'd been given, we would interview them. About future flights, there might be one but we didn't know. We were sorry, we simply had no information.

While this was going on, Sheikha looked calm, unruffled. I tried hard to look the same. But we both knew exactly what was going through people's minds as they watched those called for interviews walk up the hill to our table. "That family is getting out," they were thinking. "But what about *me*? What about *my* wife and *my* children?"

As more people came up and asked the same questions, we could feel the tension building. One young man looked straight at me and said, "What do you think is going to happen to me if you don't take me out? They're going to kill me." He had a long face, wide eyes, fine features—the stereotypical Tutsi look. He wasn't hysterical. His tone was calm and measured. He was quietly pleading for his life. "You know what's going to happen to me? You need to take me out of here."

An hour or two into the process I walked down the hill to the gray building to go to the bathroom. As I was coming back I was suddenly surrounded by four young men. They were too close, right in my face. I tensed up and looked around for the police. But they were all smiling. One of them said, "We're El Memeyi's nephews. Do you know him? Do you know anything about him?"

El Memeyi was one of the Tutsi leaders. He had been on an earlier evacuation that had gone to a UN refugee camp in Benin. I had met him there when I was preparing people from that evacuation for resettlement in the United States.

"Oh, my God," I said. "I was just with El Memeyi in Benin a little while ago."

Their eyes lit up. "Really? What's happening with him? How is he? Tell us about him."

"He's fine. He and some of your other relatives will be going to the United States soon. They're worried about you. When they heard you didn't make it onto the last flight they didn't know what to think."

I was about to tell them more—I was excited to see them and wanted to fill them in about Benin. Then out of the corner of my eye I noticed that the tall man in the fedora and sunglasses was moving closer to us, obviously trying to catch what I was saying. I quickly cut off the conversation. "Everything's fine with them, don't worry." The guy in the fedora gave me the creeps. I was getting a definite sense of menace from him. "Maybe we can talk later," I said to the nephews.

Up at the tables Sheikha was by herself. Our minders had gone off for their own break. I gestured down the hill. "That guy in the hat and sunglasses, with the ratty sport jacket. Do you see him? Do you know anything about him?"

Sheikha looked. "That bastard is going to burn in hell," she said. "He's *Interahamwe*."

I was shocked, not just by what Sheikha said but by how she said it. I had never heard her curse before.

"When they took the 112 off the buses last time, that bastard was gloating about it."

Interahamwe! I took a moment to process what it meant that we had an Interahamwe here. Interahamwe were the Hutu Power paramilitaries who carried out the Rwandan genocide. They were mass murderers. They had had plenty of help, but they were at the heart of it. When they were finally driven out of Rwanda, they reorganized in the Congo, planning to go back into Rwanda to finish what they had started. It was their presence in eastern Congo that started the giant conflagration currently tearing the country to pieces. It made me feel dirty just having one of those people here, like being in the same space with a Nazi SS officer.

Sheikha had spent so much time at the center that she knew the place inside out. People had told her about this person and about others like him. He wasn't the only bad guy who had been placed among the Tutsi refugees. They were there to do whatever damage they could—to sabotage the evacuations or spy for the Congolese security forces. Or maybe worse. Refugee camps are dangerous places. Refugees come from places in conflict, and often the conflict follows them in the form of assassins who want revenge or to permanently silence witnesses. The Hutu/Tutsi killing didn't spare people just because they happened to be in some supposedly protected camp, and this center was a shaky place with just a handful of guards, drawn from a regime that hated Tutsis.

The whole thing was a giant paradox. The Congo regime was slaughtering Tutsis right and left, but at the same time was being forced to help save at least some of them by allowing this protection center to operate.

What had shut down IOM's rescue missions was that the Congo's strongmen had seen the huge financial potential of the evacuations. Their country was coming apart. Seven African nations had armies in the Congo fighting it out for the country's vast mineral resources. Free flights out, along with potential US visas and future green cards, were worth a fortune to anybody able to pay. The intimidation and fraud had finally become too much for my boss, David Derthick, and he had told the Americans, the UN, and the ICRC that the International Organization for Migration couldn't run any more flights. Sheikha and I were handling the ground operation for this final mission, while Davide Terzi, an IOM senior emergency management person, was trying to keep the Congolese big men in line.

That was why the Interaham we were here. They had been sent in by the regime to assassinate anyone on their hit list. I only knew one intended victim for sure: Jacob Batend, one of the 112 people on our list. We hadn't registered Jacob yet; he was somewhere down there in the crowd. Jacob's name had come up time and again. David Derthick had said that if we got only one person out it had to be him. Jacob was a lawyer, one of the leaders of the Congolese Tutsis from the southeast. A gentle man, he was widely admired and beloved by his people. Before the regime decided to cleanse the country of Tutsis, Jacob had worked for the government in the president's office. When the terror started, he was in the crosshairs. Because he had been part of the government, he now had a price on his head. He was a Tutsi who knew too much.

Fortunately for Jacob Batend, his wife wasn't Tutsi. She was from a tribe that was well-connected politically, so she and their young daughter were safe. Jacob went into hiding. Sheikha had spent time with him on her earlier missions at the center and knew many of the details of his story. He spent a year moving from one hideout to another, never staying in one place for more than a couple of weeks at a time. Jacob's friends had hidden him, but people who harbored Tutsis were putting their lives and their families' lives at risk. Children were curious about the man in the attic whom they had been told was there to fast and pray. They would wonder why they weren't allowed to invite their friends over. Neighbors would become suspicious. After a while, the place would just become too dangerous and Jacob would have to move on.

Since Kinshasa was under curfew, Jacob could only be moved during the daytime. Buried under blankets and clothing in a sweltering car trunk, he had to wait until the children in the next safe house had gone to sleep. That often meant an entire day in stifling 140-degree heat.

After many months on the run, Jacob heard that his wife, who was pregnant when he fled, had given birth to another daughter. He also heard that his eldest brother had been killed along with his wife and their children, then that his second brother and his family had been killed. And that was only the beginning. His two sisters and their families, and many of his uncles, aunts, and cousins, were also among the dead. Jacob's entire extended family was all but wiped out.

It was a year into the anti-Tutsi pogrom before the ICRC, the United States, and others brought enough pressure to force the Congolese to allow a protection center. Jacob Batend found his way there, where he was reunited with his wife and two little girls. He had been on the run for thirteen months. Once in the center, as weak as he was, he had taken the lead in helping and counseling other Tutsis, many of whom had suffered tragedies as terrible or even more terrible than his own.

Jacob and his family had been scheduled to be evacuated on David and Sheikha's second mission, but at the last moment security held them back. On David's final mission, they were scheduled again. This time they were allowed to board the buses for the airport. But that last evacuation had spiraled out of control. A Kinshasa newspaper was fed information that IOM was giving out free US visas. Thousands of people mobbed the Human Rights Ministry, where David and Sheikha had often been seen. David heard that people were offering bribes to government officials houses, cars, and giant sums of money, anything to get themselves or their relatives onto the evacuation. The day before the departure date, Sheikha's main black market money contact was arrested. The pressure was so great that another IOM officer who worked with David and Sheikha buckled under it and returned to Nairobi.

When the caravan with Jacob and his wife aboard arrived at the airport, the buses were surrounded by soldiers, police, and UN and US embassy staff. Jacob got off the bus with his family and walked toward the plane. Then immigration officers grabbed him and hustled him off.

I had heard this story from Sheikha, who had been devastated. She had cried bitterly when soldiers dragged him away from his wife and daughters. When she and David followed up to see what had happened, they were told that Jacob had been taken for interrogation and was about to be hauled off to an execution site when ICRC personnel succeeded in finding him and pressuring the soldiers to return him to the protection center. I wondered exactly how they had managed that particular feat.

As far as we knew, Jacob still had a price on his head. It was possible that the Interahamwe's main goal in the protection center was to assassinate him.

That was only one reason we were keeping our mouths shut. We didn't want news to spread about timing or anything else. The ministries had our schedule, but that didn't mean the information had filtered out to the Interahamwe or any other sinister types who might have gotten into the compound. Knowing our deadlines might jolt them into action. If people with bad intentions knew when we were leaving, they could arrange for roadblocks. They could stop the buses and incite mobs to attack or arrange for some kind of militia ambush. Someone might bribe the bus company to suddenly find they had no buses available on the day we had ordered them. They could blackmail us with these or other threats. Political figures or power brokers could use the popular anti-Tutsi bloodlust to wreak havoc in a dozen ways. Unscrupulous types could sell information about when the flight was leaving along with promises to get people on it. The possibilities were endless, none of them good.

On previous evacuations, David and Sheikha's hotel phones had been bugged. They had been followed. Their rooms and things had been searched. We anticipated that this was going to be happening to us as well. I expected that my email would be monitored. We assumed our drivers were being paid off by the government to listen in on our conversations. The situation made me think of the old joke—if you're not paranoid, you must be crazy.

Jacob Batend was in the middle of our list. When we called him up, I watched to see if our ministry minders showed any signs of recognition. They didn't. Jacob was a smallish man, five-foot-eight or so, very gaunt. He smiled and answered our questions in a soft voice. Despite their history with each other, neither he nor Sheikha gave any indication that this was anything more or less than any other interview. They hardly looked at each other. A few simple questions, a few simple answers. When I took him aside for a photograph I was thinking, this is him. This is the man we are meant to get out of here whatever happens. Then he was gone down the hill, back into the crowd.

It was late in the afternoon when Sheikha and I finished the interviews. We were physically exhausted from the heat and emotionally exhausted from the imploring eyes of the many hundreds who now understood that they would not be getting out. We had registered all 112, everyone we had been sent to take out.

As we were packing up, Francois, the ICRC official, motioned us aside. "I know what you announced at the meeting yesterday, that you're only evacuating the ones who were left behind last time." He glanced at the minders. "But what is this, that IOM will not consider these other people? These women and children we just brought in. Widows, orphans. They came straight from prison, a death camp. Have you seen them?"

He gestured toward a big tent pitched near the back end of the compound's crumbling cement dormitory. "Please, they're in there. Go. See them."

Sheikha and I looked at each other. One day gone and we could already feel what was building up in this place. We had four or five hundred desperate people in front of us, only 112 of whom would be leaving for safety. All of them were Tutsis, many of them tall and thin with straight noses and narrow faces, features that were an automatic death sentence everywhere in this country but here.

Trying to get anyone else on the flight was out of the question, even assuming we could think of a way to finesse our minders or maybe find the right people to pay off. And many of those not on the list had been in the compound for a month or two already, after surviving who knew what horrors. The women and children in the tent had just arrived. How could we even think of putting them ahead of others who were here earlier and needed to get out just as badly? We were probably going to end up with a riot on our hands. Trying to take any of these new arrivals would be pouring gasoline on a fire.

"Listen," Sheikha told Francois, "you know we can't take anyone else. That's all they're allowing. We don't have a way around it."

"I understand," he said. "All I want you to do is go and see them."

I didn't want to go. I knew what I was going to see if I did. Women and children who had been through hell. We had just interviewed a hundred-plus people who had been through hell. Seeing these people in the tent would only make things worse. There was nothing we could do for them.

"Anyway," said Sheikha, "how did you find them, how did you know about them?"

"I'm not sure," said Francois. "I heard there might have been a relationship between one of the teenage girls and some military person."

"How was it that you didn't find them before?"

"They were in Kananga. In a military prison. It was an execution center. You must see them." He looked straight at Sheikha. "Go, go see them."

"No," she said. "I can't."

"Just see them. Go and look at them. They're Tutsis. Women and children. If you leave them here, what will happen? You know what will happen."

I could feel Sheikha's agitation. She was beginning to tremble. "Sasha," she said, "you stay here. I'm going to go." This was just what David said would happen. This was why he wanted me to be in charge instead of Sheikha. Sheikha was a bleeding heart, he told me. It was her one flaw. And now I was going to have to deal with her and whatever she was going to think after she saw what was down there.

TWO

YOUR VALUES IN
THE BALANCE

*Opening Your Eyes, Confronting
Yourself, Knowing Yourself*

*The price of loyalty to some values
and commitments is the sacrifice of others.*

Joseph Badaracco

People need a push.

Manfred Ket de Vries

Watching Sheikha go down the hill toward the tent, I was clear
about my own feelings. I was *not* going to see these people. I
wasn't really prepared emotionally for any of this. Even without the
women and children in the tent our situation was barely tolerable—
taking those on our list and leaving the three or four hundred others
here to their fate. But you steel yourself for these things, and something in your makeup goes along with it or buys into it. If you're a
refugee worker in crisis situations, you get used to it. I wasn't used to
it, but I was getting there.

Two summers earlier, I had been seconded to the International Organization for Migration (IOM) by the State Department. I sat in on a meeting of IOM, US, and UNHCR (The Office of the United Nations High Commissioner for Refugees) officials called to decide which group of refugees the United States should resettle first, the Somali Bantus or the so-called "Lost Boys of Sudan." What struck me at that meeting was the fact that the principals were making a decision that was going to determine the future of many thousands of lives. Both groups couldn't be resettled at the same time; the representatives there had to choose one or the other. There were maybe 15,000 Somali Bantus living in the UN's Dadaab camp on Kenya's border with Somalia and more than 6,000 Lost Boys living in semi-starvation circumstances in the Kakuma camp in Kenya's arid northwest. Which group would go to America first?

Both were ultimately deserving. The Somali Bantus were despised outsiders in Somalia where they had been brought a hundred and fifty years earlier, captured in their native Tanzania, Mozambique, and Malawi by slavers and sold off from the slave pits in Zanzibar. Ethnically distinct from Somalis, who scorned them as an inferior race, the Bantus were preyed upon by clan warlords who battled back and forth for the farmland the Bantus worked. The violence had turned the Bantu home areas into graveyards. Tens of thousands had escaped across the Kenyan border, vowing never to go back. But there was nowhere else for them to go, either. Thousands had simply melted away into East Africa's slums and byways, disappearing from the UN's refugee grid. The remnants of their diaspora had been in Dadaab for years.

The Sudanese Lost Boys were youngsters with their own unique experience of tragedy. More than 6,000 had been in the Kakuma camp for almost eight years, girls as well as boys, even though the "Lost Boy" name had stuck. They were survivors of a children's refugee exodus that, as far as I know, had no parallel in human history. A dozen years earlier, an especially vicious eruption of violence in the Sudanese civil war had destroyed large swaths of southern Sudan and generated a mass flight of children whose villages were destroyed and whose parents were killed or missing. Some of the child refugees were four or five years old; their elders were ten or eleven. They had walked for weeks, some for months, across Sudan toward Ethiopia, with no food, no water, and no protection. The death rate was horrific.

Three years later, there was a revolution in Ethiopia. The children's camps there were attacked and they were driven back into Sudan, again with tremendous loss of life. For a year they wandered through East Africa until the survivors washed up in Kakuma. Their home areas were a wasteland, and there was no country in Africa that would take them in. I had worked with them in Kakuma. "This is a darkness place," one of them told me. I had been in Dadaab too, as isolated and dangerous a camp as any in the UN system. It was hard to believe that people could actually survive there.

In the end, the decision came down to the quality of documentation that existed for the two groups. The Bantus were almost all undocumented; the Sudanese had been registered by the UN and several NGOs when they originally crossed into Ethiopia as children. Since refugees have to be verified and documented before they can be resettled, and the job of documenting the Bantus was going to be massive, the decision was made to take the Lost Boys first.

Nothing untoward happened at the meeting; it was a careful, rational discussion. But it highlighted for me the power decision makers in this field have over people's lives—literally over life and death. The fact that the Sudanese Lost Boys were chosen to go first meant that hundreds more Bantu women were going to be raped. Others would be attacked and killed. Terrible things had been happening to those Somali Bantus as the documentation process wore on. That didn't

mean the Lost Boy decision was wrong. Their lives and futures too
would have changed dramatically if the Bantus had gone first.

The lesson here wasn't about right and wrong. The lesson was
about power and how to use it. That meeting helped me understand
the work I had gotten myself into. Here was a world of competing
demands in circumstances that meant life for some and death for others. How are you supposed to act when you have that kind of power?

That meeting was a cornerstone for me. It drove home how important it was to keep right in the forefront of my mind that I could so
easily be in the place of the person I'm trying to help. You're looking
at a list of strange-sounding names, but that list isn't just a list. Each
of those names is a human being with loved ones and with the same
feelings you have. You have to consider them that way, even though
all you know of them is a name on a printed sheet. And the fact is, you
just do not necessarily think like that. You think about the numbers.
You think about what's easier to do and what's the most efficient way
to do it. That's how the principals at the meeting thought about it and
discussed it. And now here I was, a year and a half later, with a list
of life and death in my own hands, with the same kind of decision
to make—much smaller in scope, but even more complicated. And
there was my colleague heading off down the hill to complicate things
even further.

I thought I knew what was going on in Sheikha's head, but years
later, in preparation for this book, we asked Sheikha explicitly about
it. Here's what she said:

> I felt like I was being pulled. On one hand, I wanted to see
> them, on the other, I was scared to go. We had the list, that was
> it. Should I, should I not? I was so curious, but what would
> happen if I did see them? Why start up something that will be
> killing me inside? David Derthick was on one side—what he
> had said about keeping to the list. But even when he said it, I

knew it would break my heart. And there was Sasha—now he was in David's place. I was torn.

But something pulled me. I just had to. "Okay," I said. "Let me just go and see."

Outside the tent I saw a little girl, painfully thin. And another slightly older but also emaciated, her little belly protruding. They were each holding something, dolls, I thought. I said to the first one, "Let me see your doll." But when I bent down to look, it wasn't a doll. It was a human baby. They were both human babies. They looked like newborns. You could see their veins, human faces. I was horrified. They were wrapped in filthy swaddling. Their heads wobbled, their skin was gray, withered, like old men. I thought, who could give these babies to other babies? "Don't let their heads wobble," I said. "Hold the backs of their necks." These little kids themselves were in awful shape. One was a toddler, the other a little older. It was just shocking.

I went inside the tent. I saw these tall, tall children, severely malnourished, a terrible sadness in their faces. I said "Habari," in Swahili. Nothing else. I couldn't speak. These people were like walking shadows. Shadows of human beings. People who had suffered and had given in to their suffering, had resigned themselves to it. Dark circles around their eyes. Haunted looks, or just blank stares. All these women, all these kids. I looked at one lady, she didn't even see me. Another one, totally withdrawn. These people were in shock. And there were so many kids, too many. A teenage boy with a baby strapped to his back and other kids around him. Hardly even human, something vital had gone out of them.

Where were they? Where had they been? What had happened to them? I went out of the tent. Francois was standing there.

"Did you see them?"

"Yes."

"What did you think?"

I didn't answer, I just walked back up the hill. I thought, this is going to kill me. We have the list, and now we have this.

I went up to Sasha. I said, "I think you should go, just have a look at them. Just see them. I want you to just see them."

"I want to tell you what happened," I said. "I saw this ema-ciated little kid outside the tent, maybe two or three years old. She was carrying a doll. I asked her if I could see it. Sasha, it wasn't a doll, it was a human baby, a shriveled little human baby. That child wasn't much more than an infant herself, and she was carrying an infant. And that was before I went into the tent. Sasha, you need to come and see this."

When Sheikha said, "You need to see this," my answer was, "There's no way. You know we just cannot do it." But as I said this, I had already started with her toward the tent, Francois, the ICRC person, trailing behind us. I didn't want to see these new people in the worst way, but I couldn't help it. It just seemed I needed to.

The tent was big, maybe twenty by twenty. Inside it was stifling. It smelled of must and decayed canvas. A few dozen people were sitting on the ground, two or three women and groups of ragged, sticklike children. No one said a word. No one seemed to be moving; the tent was impossibly still and silent. It was as if these people were the shades of the departed waiting silently to cross the river of death.

Off to one side was a woman with a cluster of children crowded around her. The woman and the children were skeletal, bones pro-truding from frail bodies. Some of the little ones had orange hair, the color of starvation, their bellies distended by hunger. Their eyes were vacant, hollow, like the eyes in pictures I'd seen of Holocaust survivors. The woman held two ragged bundles in her arms, pinched little faces poking out of the rags. Newborns. You could see the veins spiderlike under their scalps, their heads wobbling on necks that wouldn't support them. The mother seemed barely aware that we were standing there. Sheikha asked her in Swahili, "How old are your babies?"

She looked up. "*Miezi tisa*," she said, her voice a hoarse whisper. *Miezi tisa*—nine months. I wasn't sure I had heard right. How could these tiny infants be nine months old?

"All these people were in prison for sixteen months," Francois said. "One of the execution prisons. We have no idea how they survived. These infants were born there. They're supposed to be nine months old."

I looked at the mother. I looked at all the children.

We had just finished interviewing people whose family members had been massacred, who had themselves been raped, tortured, hunted. They had been at the protection center for a month or two, where at least there was food and some semblance of security. This woman and her children had just escaped from prison. They were fragile, traumatized, famished; they were at death's door. The others we were going to leave behind weren't likely to survive, but there wasn't any question about these people. They were almost gone already.

We counted them. Three women with children. One teenage head of family. Thirty-two in all. We exchanged a few words with the other women. The teenager with the baby on his back didn't reply when I said hello. He looked catatonic. I was standing right in front of him, but his mind was obviously somewhere else. "His name is Daniel," said a little boy standing next to him, holding his hand. "He doesn't talk. I can talk for him."

"Daniel's taking care of four kids," Francois said. "This one and three others."

"Daniel," I said again. "*Bonjour. Comment tu vas?*"

Nothing. I wasn't sure he even saw me.

There were a dozen other things on the agenda that had to be taken care of quickly. Tomorrow was Monday. Departure day was Thursday. That gave us three days to hire the buses and the armed guards, get stamped approvals from the Ministry of Human Rights and the Immigration Department, and make final arrangements with UNHCR in Cameroon. We wanted to limit our time in the protection center. Ideally we didn't want to go back until Thursday to get everyone on the buses. Any further appearances would just jack up the desperation and anger.

But besides all that, what were we going to do about the thirty-two women and children in that tent? We had to put it out of our minds until we had time to talk in private.

Across the way I saw Captain Jose of the compound's police squad. He was the one who had arranged the armed escort for the previous flights. David Derthick had told me to go back to him for this one as well. David had also warned me against hiring too much security. For the previous evacuation he had had almost thirty guards, but David thought thirty guns were just too many. They turned things more volatile, he said, more dangerous rather than less. I thought it would make sense to have two guards per bus. I was going to rent four buses, three for everyone who was going and a backup in case of a breakdown or some other problem.

I told the captain, "We're taking three vehicles. I need two guards per vehicle. That's six. Plus you. We'll pay the same as last time."

"Six?" he said, surprised. "We had thirty last time."

"Right. This time we only need six—plus yourself."

"Six is very little," he said. "This is dangerous work." (I was sure he was taking kickbacks on the payments, in addition to his own cut.) "With only six we'll need more money than last time."

Much more, as it turned out. But I agreed, this wasn't something to start bargaining over. We needed this man's cooperation.

The car ride back took an hour. Sheikha and I wanted badly to talk, but we were pretty sure the driver was a government plant, so we kept our mouths shut. We were staying at the Memling Hotel, one of Kinshasa's two first-class hotels. The Memling's posh, marbled lobby included a collection of expensive boutiques on one side. Toward the back was a fancy buffet area and beyond that was an outdoor swimming pool built into an expansive stone patio. The Memling would have fit right in as a four-star hotel in Miami or Los Angeles.

Or it would have if it weren't for the guests. The Congo was full of arms traffickers, smugglers, diamond and gold dealers—every type of shady person you can imagine who might be drawn to a lawless country where there is untold wealth and great violence and they could make a fortune. The Congo attracted the underbelly of the world. And a lot of that underbelly seemed to be staying at the Memling, or at least doing business there. Prostitutes strolled in and out dressed in skin-tight miniskirts and skimpy, revealing blouses. The lobby's male guests flaunted gold on their necks and Rolexes on their wrists. On our way to the elevator we passed an immensely fat man on one of the lobby sofas, who reminded me of Jabba the Hutt. He was deep in conversation with several other questionable types in dark suits and sunglasses. It was a very seedy scene.

Our suite was on the top floor. It featured a grandiose foyer that opened onto a large living room with a wall of windows overlooking the city, whose northern edge was bounded by the Congo River, a huge, sinuous anaconda flowing majestically toward the Atlantic. It was easy to imagine Kinshasa's kleptocrat elite staying in this place.

We both went off to wash up. I was steeling myself for a battle with Sheikha, which was making me feel extremely uncomfortable. Sheikha and I had been friends almost from the moment I had set

foot in IOM's Nairobi office half a year before. We always seemed
to have something to talk about, and, over the past months, it was
usually the earlier Congo evacuations that were taking every ounce
of her emotional energy. Coming back from the Congo with David
Derthick between missions, she'd unburden herself to me, telling me
about the traumatized refugees, the government thugs, the spies, the
close calls with mobs. Her stories were riveting. And when I returned
from working with the evacuees in Benin and Cameroon, I was able
to give her news about many of the people she had helped rescue.

Sheikha was David's right hand. Of all his operations officers,
there was no one he knew better or appreciated more. But when it
came to the list, I knew David was right to be concerned about her.
The problem with Sheikha was her huge heart. She was a cool thinker,
very levelheaded, but she was by nature unable to deny herself to people in need. If someone needed money, Sheikha would reach into her
pocket. If they needed some other kind of help, she'd give it without
stinting. She was a humanitarian through and through.

David was what I thought of as a model leader in humanitarian
work. He was a man of great compassion, but he was also a hard-
shell West Virginian, the kind of person who could stand up to all
the intimidation and fraud. David would bend when necessary, but
he could also stonewall and bluff and threaten. He did what had to
be done. He knew he could talk to Sheikha till he was blue in the face
about keeping to the list, but he knew that if she came across needy
cases who were not on the list she'd try everything she could to get
them on.

Like David, Sheikha had an iron will, but her iron will was always in service to what David called her bleeding heart. Sheikha was
Swahili. Her mom was Kenyan, her father from Yemen. She had the
light brown skin of the Swahili people, and her warmth and friendli-
ness could easily come across as softness. But people who knew her

found out differently. When she was sixteen her family had married her off according to Yemeni custom, but very soon into the marriage she had decided she wasn't going to have anything to do with this person who was supposed to be her husband. She rejected him and carved out her own way, something almost unheard of among Muslim women and especially for someone who was little more than a girl.

By the time I met her, Sheikha was in her early thirties, living with her mom and her two children, Ismail and Maida. How those children came to her was another story. Ismail had been abandoned as an infant and was taken in by an older Muslim woman who then died. Sheikha and her mother had been asked by the religious community to help with the body, and in the dead woman's room they found a naked three-month-old baby tangled up in the bedsheets on the floor. When they couldn't locate any of the dead woman's relatives, they simply kept the child themselves.

Several years later two policemen came to Sheikha's door with a tiny bundle of rags. Inside the bundle was a premature newborn hunched in the fetal position. The baby, a girl, was the size of a Coke bottle and weighed two pounds. The police had found the infant in an empty room in a building housing refugees. No one knew who the mother was. They had first taken the baby to the national hospital, but they debated whether they should bring her in. She was obviously too premature to live without a lot of attention—and probably not then either. With no one to claim her, the police knew the hospital would just let her die and dump the body. Then they thought of Sheikha. Sheikha had taken that other abandoned baby, maybe she would take this one too.

Maida was now a precocious five-year-old ball of energy. Her brother, Ismail, was an equally bright nine. Knowing their stories was all anyone had to know about Sheikha herself. This was not a woman who was about to deny someone in need, someone whose name might not appear on a list.

Of course, David had put his worries about Sheikha on my shoulders. I had no doubt she would want to figure out some scheme to take the widows and orphans. I knew I was going to have to fight this out with her, and I was gearing myself up for it. I was the junior person here, but David trusted me, which gave me confidence that I was up to it, whatever Sheikha's attitude might be. Or Davide Terzi's either. Terzi was going to show up here in a while, to brief us on his day with the regime strongmen. I had no idea what he might think. But the operational side of this was in our hands, Sheikha's and mine, and my business here was to protect the list and make sure we succeeded in taking out the people we had come to take out.

Davide Terzi arrived later that evening to brief us on his day with the regime strongmen at the various ministries and with the embassy contact group. He wanted to tell us about it, but the widows and orphans couldn't wait. They were preying on our minds, Sheikha's and mine. Those impossibly tiny infants. Their mother. The other mothers. The boy who couldn't speak. Everyone in that tent.

Sheikha switched the TV on, turning the volume way up. From the moment we started describing what we had seen, Terzi understood. He'd been through a lot in his career. No doubt he'd seen more than a few people in the same state.

We all felt the same way. We *should* take these people out. They were practically dead already. No question what would happen if we left them there. But we had already been adamant with the US embassy, the Ministry of Human Rights, the embassy contact group, the Congo Immigration Department. They all knew where we stood on the numbers. Not only that, Terzi said, the Ministry of Human Rights had leaned on the US embassy to take five more cases. He had been forced to agree to that. He had also heard from the contact group embassies, the Swiss, the French, the Belgians. They too were starting to lobby for us to take their special cases, Tutsi employees they were hiding. Terzi understood we had had an interesting day. That was *his* interesting day.

I could see the whole thing collapsing. We all could. If we decided to try taking the widows and orphans, this already delicate situation would almost certainly slip into chaos.

But regardless, after some back and forth, it seemed clear to me that Terzi wanted to try it. The man was a risk-taker. Certain risks are worth it, he said, and this was one of them. Maybe he was right, but I wasn't comfortable with either him or his judgment. He had flown to Kinshasa through Kenya, but he was only in Nairobi's Jomo Kenyatta Airport long enough to change planes. There hadn't been time for David Derthick to brief him. That meant he knew nothing about how David had navigated these waters for the six months of the first evacuations, about the mines set to explode if we strayed anywhere near them.

Looking for some direction, we called David in Nairobi and explained what was happening. But we didn't get very far before David, always so calm and deliberate, exploded. "You just cannot take anybody else!" he shouted. "It will not work! I told you this before you left! You'll screw up the entire mission and nobody will get out. Here's what's going to happen if you try this. Those bastards are going to say to you, 'You can take those people out'—and then they'll force you to include more of their own people. Then at the last minute they'll hold back the people they said *you* could take out. They did that before. They'll hold them back, and you'll be left with frauds you shouldn't have agreed to in the first place. The whole thing will go to hell. You are going to have 112 dead people on your conscience—forever! Is that what you want? *Just do not do it!*"

I took a deep breath. Okay, I thought. He's right, and I'm supposed to be the one holding the fort here. I began seeing dead people
whichever way I turned, no matter what we decided. If we did try to
take the thirty-two, we'd lose what little control we had. We'd have
zero ground to stand on when the Congolese big men demanded that
we add their cronies and frauds to our evacuation list, which they
would do, which they had already started doing. We'd face demands
we couldn't refuse, yet couldn't meet. And what then?

Sticking to our list—plus the five extra ministry cases now—was
the only way we could possibly maintain our ability to manage this
thing. It was all so fragile and volatile. Who knew what this kind of
disruption to our plan would bring? I saw a black pit opening up,
swirling with violence and chaos. I thought about the mobs throng-
ing around the Ministry of Human Rights, the Hutu Power killers
working away at whatever malevolence they had in mind. The protection center itself was a powder keg of desperation. Letting go of our
control meant opening ourselves up to the unforeseen, probably the
catastrophic. It would be like turning the headlights off, pressing the
pedal to the metal, and letting go of the steering wheel in the middle
of the night on a dark road.

I had seen the widows and orphans. No one had to tell me about
them. But it wasn't as if the 112 we had come to rescue were just
names on a list. Even before I met them, I tried to stay focused on
their individuality, and now I had met them all. I'd taken their pictures, seen their children, asked about their families. Jacob Batend,
for one. Or El Memeyi's four nephews, so full of smiles and eager to
join him and their brothers in the Benin transit camp. That father and
son who had been torn away from their family the last time. What
was it the father had whispered? "Please hurry. This is a dangerous
place." All their hopes were on our shoulders. Theirs and the hopes of

all the others we had interviewed, whose faces were in my head even if I couldn't put every picture to every name.

We owed it to each of them to play this as carefully as possible, not to risk their lives because of our own weakness. David had given us a clear road map. We needed to stick with that, to play this coldly, conservatively, rationally. That was our best chance to save anyone.

My whole professional life I had wanted to understand what refugees went through and do what I could to help save lives. And here I was, here we were, right in the middle of it. Here I wasn't just working with survivors; I was inside their experience, in the very center of their crisis, and at the center of my own crisis too. Every person in the compound was filled with dread. Death was all around them, waiting for them. Death had already claimed many of their family and friends; now it was coming after them. And here we were, arbiters of life and death. Sheikha, Terzi, and I.

"You know," I said to Terzi, "I understand there are nuances to this. I understand there's a delicate balance with these thugs we're dealing with. I understand that you're the one with the experience. But you do not know what's gone on here for the last six months. You heard David on the phone. If we try to take these people, we are going to get everyone killed. We're going to lose them all. You understand that, right? I want to take them as badly as you do, but we just cannot do it."

Terzi wasn't having any of it. I could see he had made his decision and wasn't going to entertain my thoughts about it, or David Derthick's either. "Stop worrying it," he told me. "Stop trying to overthink it. Everything you're saying at this point is just for the benefit of your own conscience. You've got to stop it."

Okay, that's Terzi, I thought. But he's not calling the shots on this. Sheikha and I are, and David back in Nairobi, whose operation this whole thing was, anyway.

I knew I was throwing down the gauntlet with Sheikha. I knew
Sheikha. I knew what was inside her head. But I didn't know everything.
I definitely knew I couldn't see this situation properly. I felt completely
inadequate to do that, to weigh the value of lives like this. But David
could. Who better? I had been working with him for six months now,
ever since I arrived in Africa. I had never met anyone so competent,
so grounded, so cool in his judgments. Maybe I wasn't up to making a
judgment here, but he was. He had been involved in this kind of thing
for years, deciding issues that meant salvation for some and not for others. Life and death resting on his shoulders. Maybe I didn't know what
to do, but David was a lodestar I could follow. Besides being my boss.

But Sheikha had her own ideas, and, without my knowing it, she
was already handling this in her own way.

Here is Sheikha again, looking back on that night.

*All the way back from the protection center to Kinshasa my
head was spinning. I was watching Sasha, thinking about how
to fight with him. When we got back, without Sasha knowing, I
called Davide Terzi. I told him about the widows and orphans.
"We can't go without them. This operation is exactly for people
like them. We have to do what we have to do. You have to talk
to Sasha. You have to work on him. How can we leave them?
How can we not include them?"*

*Terzi said, "But the plane is full. The list plus the five extra
the ministry's forcing us to take—that's almost capacity."*

"Don't worry," I told him. "We'll take care of that."

"How?"

*"We'll do it. Don't worry, we'll figure it out." In reality I had
no idea. We'd think of something.*

"Okay," he said. "I'll talk with him."

*I had to do that. It wasn't to disrespect Sasha. It was a way
to start it going. I knew if we all agreed together, Terzi, me, and*

Sasha, then David Derthick was the only other person, and the three of us together would be able to overcome him. We were here. He was in Nairobi, 1,000 miles away.

That night at the hotel, I was fighting with Sasha about taking the widows and orphans. When it got to be too over-whelming I would rush to the bathroom and cry. I would talk to the mirror, practicing how I could speak to him without be-ing too emotional. I didn't want to show that I was hysterical or overwhelmed. I wanted to convince him. I would cry and cry, then compose myself. But I was dying inside. I was burning inside. I went back again and again and talked to the mirror. I asked God, "Please give me strength so that when I talk I won't sound like a useless, emotional person, not making good judgments. So he won't think I'm just an emotional, distraught woman. So he'll see that what I'm saying makes sense."

Eating, we couldn't eat. Sleeping, we couldn't sleep. I un-derstood that Sasha had to respect his orders from David. And even though he felt what I was feeling, he had strict instruc-tions. So what was going to persuade him? What was the best way to handle this?

I said to him, "It will be senseless that we are carrying people who have been put there by the ministry, who don't de-serve to be there, and we are not going to take these women and children. How can we do that? Take those who have been planted on us, and not these? What justice is that? If this is not for them, then who is this for? What are we here for? Are we humanitarians or are we not?"

We didn't sleep. We talked and talked. I was ready to stand up to Terzi. My assessment of him was that he was the kind of person who would take things to the edge out of gut instinct and an inclination to hazard the odds. A gambler. I wasn't in that camp. That wasn't the way to make this decision. Not for me anyway. Sheikha was a different story. Sheikha's bottom line was compassion. You do everything you can for those in need. You put yourself on the line for them. You do not give up, no matter what, even if it means you yourself might go down with the ship. That's where she was coming from with the women and children in the tent. We might end up with a disaster on our hands. She wasn't disregarding the lives we might lose, and what that would mean for us personally. I could just imagine the regret, the guilt, the awful psychological consequences. But that didn't mean we could give up on women and children who so desperately needed us. *"Are we humanitarians or are we not?"* That got to me. It crushed every defense I had left. Am I a humanitarian or am I not? Was I a human being committed to the welfare of my fellow human beings? What were my own instincts telling me, the bottom line of my own nature? Not what David Derthick was telling me. Not what some rational moral calculus was saying about weighing this quantity of lives against that quantity.

That's what dawned on me as the hours went on. And that's where I finally ended up. "Okay," I told Sheikha finally. "Let's figure out a way to take them."

We called David Derthick again. This time his tone was different. Despite everything he had put into this Tutsi rescue operation—his whole heart and soul—he had obviously been thinking it over. He knew we were seeing things he wasn't. This mission just wasn't his anymore. "All right," he said. "It's your operation. But whatever you do, first you have to clear it with the US embassy. If they say it's okay, it's okay with me."

THREE

TAKE COURAGE

Making the Decision,
Implementing It

We are not the heroes. The heroes are the
survivors who endured torture, genocide, and
all the pain, and yet they had faith and hope.

Sheikha Ali

It was almost morning before Terzi left and Sheikha and I went off
to our bedrooms to try to catch an hour's sleep. When we got up,
Sheikha called the US embassy to get approval for what we were going to do. The ambassador, William Swing, was away, but she got
hold of our contact there, Barry, the chargé d'affaires, who said he'd
be in touch with Swing and get back to us. "They're both good guys,"
Sheikha told me. "They'll okay it. Let's not worry about them."

I wasn't worried about them. My mind wasn't on the embassy. It
was on how we could register the widows and orphans without the
whole place blowing up, which we had to do by tomorrow at the latest. Of course, even with the embassy's approval we'd still need to deal
with the Human Rights minister. Terzi would have to handle him

somehow. That wasn't in our venue. All Sheikha and I had to do was figure out the registering, and we were running out of time for that fast.

Neither of us was eager to go out to the protection center, but the five cases the Human Rights minister had foisted on us were going to arrive there and we'd need to document them. I also wanted to confirm the armed guard arrangements with Jose, the police captain, and try to see the widows and orphans again. Maybe I could start figuring out how to get them on our manifest in the face of the hundreds we were leaving behind.

A crowd formed the moment we drove through the compound's big black doors. All eyes were riveted on Sheikha as she made her way up the hill to where our two minders were already sitting. I stayed in the car until Sheikha was halfway up. No one paid any attention to me as I walked over to Captain Jose and asked if he would come with me to the big tent. The only one who seemed to notice was the Interahamwe in the fedora who swiveled around to look, his eyes hidden behind the dark glasses.

Inside the tent it was just as close and stifling as it had been yesterday. Near me was fifteen-year-old Daniel, the one who wouldn't speak. I said hello and asked him how he was. He just stared, though this time at least it seemed he knew I was talking to him. One of the little kids next to him took his hand and looked up at me. I was surprised when he said in halting English, "My name is Pitchu." I looked down at him, "Hi, Pitchu, how are you?" then repeated it in French when it was clear he didn't understand. "Hi. How are you? And how is your big brother Daniel here?"

"Okay," the little boy said, looking at Daniel, who was all too obviously not okay.

The woman with the infants was sitting in what looked like exactly the same place, in the same position, cradling a bundle in each arm. I wondered if she had moved at all since yesterday. The other children were still close to her, seven of them. I went over and smiled, squatting down to look more closely at the babies. It was almost beyond belief that they were nine months old. They were tiny, completely helpless. Their skin seemed gray rather than brown, almost translucent. I wanted to tell the mother that we were going to get them out of here. That we would fly her to someplace safe where doctors could take care of her and her babies. But I only said hi. I tried to convey with my eyes the determination I was feeling, even as I understood how pointless that was. Who knew if we *could* actually get them out of here?

I left the tent and looked up the hill. Five people were sitting in front of Sheikha—the ministry cases. I climbed the hill and began taking pictures. When we were done, I leaned over to Sheikha and whispered, "What should we do about the thirty-two?"

"Not now," she whispered back. "It's getting too dangerous. See what's going on down there?" She gave a quick nod toward the crowd. "They aren't happy about these five we just did."

I gestured down to Captain Jose that we wanted to get to our car. Sheikha and I joined him and a couple of other police in an informal cluster that moved quickly toward where the car was parked. The people didn't crowd us, but they formed a kind of loose moving circle. "Why them?" we heard. "If you're taking them, you have to take us." "Answer us!" someone shouted. "Why not us and our children?"

That night Sheikha and I talked about how we could get the thirty-two out. Tomorrow was Tuesday. Evacuation was Thursday. We needed a final list of evacuees ASAP. A complete list had to go to the Cameroon government. Cameroon Airlines, our carrier, needed the passenger manifest. Congo Immigration would need to check names and photos. UNHCR needed to document all entrants to the Cameroon refugee camp. The US Joint Voluntary Agency needed names and numbers to set up their immigration interviews. So, how were we going to do this?

We knew we couldn't just call thirty-two people up for interviews at our usual place on the hill. There was no telling how the crowd might react to that. But where else could we do it? If Sheikha and I disappeared inside the tent, word would spread immediately. We talked about what could happen. Anger could trigger a riot of some sort, and if things turned violent all bets were off. There were six, maybe seven police in the compound. They could start shooting people. The crowd could turn on them. That sinister Interahamwe character could use the confusion to assassinate Jacob Batend. Any kind of serious incident would abort the evacuation and leave everyone in the center to the tender mercies of the Congolese.

The trick would be to use some kind of ploy, maybe something about health. The widows and orphans had just come out of sixteen months in a death camp, and they looked it. They were far worse off than anyone else. Maybe we could do medical checks, or at least use that as a cover for seeing them. We could say we needed to do health evaluations. Maybe we could use the building to do that, the gray cement building in the middle of the compound. Some of the center refugees were living in there—there were small rooms and a row of hole toilets. But there was also a little room that Captain Jose used as his office. We could have him bring one family at a time there. I could register and photograph them. Meanwhile, Sheikha could sit at the table on the hill as usual, in full view, doing some kind of make-work, maybe with one of the ICRC officers. That would be our diversion.

The next morning, we drove into the center. No crowds surrounded us this time, but people were watching, warily. The place was thick with tension.

Sheikha and I walked to the top of the hill. Our two minders were there, as usual. We had a little discussion, then I excused myself as discreetly as I could. The police had arrayed themselves at the bottom of the hill, and I motioned to Captain Jose that I wanted to talk. The crowd had gathered, but everything seemed unusually quiet. No one was paying any attention to me. All eyes were on the tables at the top of the hill.

I told Jose what I had in mind. I wanted to use his office. I wanted him to spread the word quietly that the people in the tent needed medical evaluations. "No announcements. Just have one or two of your men tell a few people. The word will spread. Then I'd like you to bring one family at a time in there so I can interview them and take their pictures."

Jose led me inside to his office, a small space, but big enough for what I had to do. I sat down at his desk and waited. I was sure the word was already starting to go around about the health checks. People would hear it, but they'd hardly pay any attention. They were too wound up, too concentrated on Sheikha and the others up on the hill.

A few minutes later there was a knock on the door and a police-man ushered in one of the widows and eight children, several in their teens, the youngest a toddler. I said hello and introduced myself. I told her I needed to get details about her and her children—names and ages—and I was going to take their pictures. I began to explain that we were going to try to get her family out of the center, but there were many people here whom we would not be able to take out. So it was important that neither she nor any of her children should say anything to anyone about our interview.

I was halfway through this explanation when the door banged open and three large men barged into the room. The leader was wearing some kind of uniform, though I wasn't sure what. He wasn't police, he wasn't a soldier, but he was something official, and he was angry. He slammed the door shut and glared at me. The woman and children shrank into a corner. It felt like the three men were taking up all the available space.

I opened my mouth but didn't have a chance to get a word out. "What do you think you're doing?" the leader barked. "Who gave you permission to talk to these people?"

I began explaining that I had to take photos and get some information, but he cut me off. "You're not in charge here! We need to interview this family. I want you to leave right now!"

I looked toward the corner. The woman's eyes were begging me not to go.

"No. You see," I started, "I need to talk to them to get—"

He cut me off again. He moved up to the desk and leaned on it, putting his face close to mine. "Now is the time for you to go and do your other work," he growled. "Let us take care of business here."

I picked up my papers and my camera and walked out slowly, glancing at the woman and children as I left. I didn't even know who these guys were. But it was pretty clearly not in anyone's interest for me to start arguing with them.

I climbed the hill and sat down next to Sheikha. I looked down at the crowd, still quiet, but I knew exactly what was going through their heads. They were all thinking what that one man had shouted yesterday: *Why not us and our kids?*

'These three guys came into Jose's office," I said to Sheikha. "I was talking to the first family, but they wouldn't let me do it. They told me to leave. I didn't feel I had a choice."

"I saw them," Sheikha said. "They're government security. You don't argue with them, but we have to get that registration data. I think I know what to do here. Tomorrow morning I'll pay them off, tell them we're hiring them to help us register the thirty-two. Let's see if we can't get them on our side."

Tomorrow would truly be the last day for that. I didn't know how we were going to work it. Our safety margins had worn away to nothing.

When Jose escorted us to the car, the crowd around us was quieter than it had been yesterday, but it was an ominous quiet. I could feel the menace.

There wasn't any choice now. Tomorrow was Wednesday. Thursday was departure. We needed to register the thirty-two. The medical check business wasn't going to work a second time. No more games. We were just going to have to do it and risk whatever might happen. Not up on the hill, though, in plain sight. That would be too much for people to bear. They'd tear the place apart. We'd use Captain Jose's office again, have the police bring in one family at a time, the same as I was doing before security threw me out.

We heard that after we left security had called all the families from the tent in for interviews, God only knew why. But now everyone in the center knew something was going on—the new arrivals were being given special attention, which could only mean one thing. They were going on the flight. We could only hope the police would be able to control things tomorrow. I don't know if Sheikha slept that night. I didn't.

Wednesday morning. The moment we drove through the gates, people gathered around the car. As Sheikha and I got out, the shouting started. "Are you taking them with you? Are you taking them? Why are you killing us?" Sheikha said, "Sasha, this isn't good. Please stay close to me." The police were around us as we all moved toward the gray building. The whole place seemed primed to go off.

Sheikha and I went into Jose's office and sat down at the desk. We had told the police to start bringing in the thirty-two, one family group at a time. As we waited for the first arrivals, some people from the crowd outside managed to shove past the police guard at the door. They wanted Sheikha. They clustered around her. "Who's on the list?" "Can you include us? Sheikha, please. Can't you put us on the list? Sheikha, you know us." They were grasping at straws and Sheikha was their last straw—Sheikha with her compassionate nature, her bleeding heart. Sheikha was strong enough to stand up to threats, to provocations, to all the regime thugs she and David Derthick had faced off with for months. But turning down people pleading for their lives was something else. She looked stricken.

They didn't know me, these people. I was just somebody who had been here for a few days with Sheikha. I started yelling at her, in English, "Get these people out of here! Get them out!" I wanted to come across as the authority, the bad cop. If they see me yelling at Sheikha, I thought, they'll think I'm in control. They'll know she doesn't have a choice—she can't save them. "Out! I want you to get them out now!"

Sheikha said nothing while the police guard came in and herded the people out. A moment later another policeman showed up with the first family, the woman with the dying twins and seven other children. Suddenly we were by ourselves in the office, just me, Sheikha, and the family. We got their names, their ages. I took their pictures. The second family arrived, another mother and seven children. Then a third widow and her eight children. Then the silent boy, Daniel, and the four children he was caring for, including little Pitchu who had spoken to me in English. Once we had registered them all and taken their pictures, we told the door guards to call Captain Jose to get us back to the car. Now was the crucial moment. If violence was going to happen, it would happen now, when we stepped out of the office into the crowd.

People crowded around us as we moved toward the car in the little cordon of police Jose had mustered. But the anger seemed to have drained out of them. Instead there was a kind of sad desperation. Many seemed resigned to the fact that they were just not getting out. Whatever their fate was going to be, it was going to be here. One Tutsi man reached out and put his hand on my shoulder. "Isn't there any way you can take me?" he said. I shook my head. "The ICRC is looking at what else they can do," I said. Then we were in the car and gone. If we can get those thirty-two out, I kept saying to myself, that will be a huge accomplishment. But it wasn't a lot of comfort.

Once we were back at the Memling, Sheikha went off to meet with Terzi, who wanted her to come with him to see the Human Rights minister, the man whose permission we needed in order to take the thirty-two. Under ordinary circumstances, the right size bribe might do it, probably too big for us to handle, but we had just accepted his additional five cases, which I was sure involved a big payoff for him and probably some of his cronies. He might be in an accommodating mood.

With Sheikha gone, I went up to our rooms to try to deal with our list of evacuees—actually two lists now, one that included the thirty-two and one that didn't, in case Terzi and Sheikha couldn't get anywhere with the minister. The first list included the original 112 and the five ministry cases. That was 117 evacuees who would be going plus Sheikha and me and an IOM doctor who had flown in and would be joining us at the protection center. Terzi was flying off to another emergency, so he wouldn't be coming with us. The 117 plus the three of us made 120. The second list included the thirty-two, which would bring the total to 152. The plane only had 126 seats, a figure we hadn't let out to anybody. Could we squeeze more people on if necessary? No, our charter was from Cameroon Air, a legitimate carrier. They'd go strictly by flight safety regulations.

For David's first evacuation they had a charter from some fly-by-night airline—Air Kazakhstan, I seemed to recall. Back then IOM couldn't get any of the legitimate airlines to fly a charter in here. The Air Kazakhstan plane was ancient. The airline didn't even have money for fuel. In order to get out of Kinshasa, David had had to pay to re-fuel the plane himself. If I had Air Kazakhstan, now I could probably get the extras on, no problem. They wouldn't care about any overload. But I didn't have Air Kazakhstan.

So, how to get the number down to 126? First, children under two would be allowed to sit in parents' laps, so they wouldn't need seats. I counted the under-twos on the original list—only three of them. There were four, maybe five under-twos among the widows and orphans: the two infants, the two toddlers, maybe one other. If we had eight altogether, that meant we'd still need seats for 144. How was I going to pare eighteen more from the manifest? I couldn't think.

Then it struck me. Why not fudge the ages of kids two and older? Change birth dates around and make all the two- and three-year-olds into one-year-olds? I did that, but I was still ten seats over. Then I changed the four-year-olds into one-year-olds. When I worked the numbers, that did it. I was down to exactly 126. Perfect. Of course, some of those one-year-olds would be awfully large. I made a mental note to tell the parents what I'd done so they would know what to say if anyone asked them. If someone questioned how a one-year-old could look like a four-year-old, they'd just have to say that the child had always been big for its age. That wouldn't stand up for a minute if someone wanted to make a case of it, but it was the best I could think of.

When I finished with the lists I went off to the City Train Bus Company to meet the manager and finalize the arrangements we had already talked over by phone. David Derthick and Sheikha had used City Train a couple of times before, so the deal here was more or less routine. I needed four buses—three for evacuees, armed guards, and ourselves, one extra for emergencies. On the theory that nothing in Kinshasa ever works the way you expect it to, I wanted to make sure I saw the City Train manager face to face so we could establish at least something in the way of a relationship. If a problem popped up, I wanted him to know who he was dealing with, what our potential was to make trouble for him, and also that I was prepared to make his life a little sweeter.

By the time I got back to the hotel, the sun was setting over Kinshasa. From my seventh floor view, the city seemed to glow an ominous red. Sheikha had left to meet Terzi at four and they still weren't back, even though the meeting shouldn't have lasted more than an hour. That was worrisome. What was happening over there? I had met the minister briefly the day we arrived, a fire hydrant of a man with exaggerated shoulders. Formidable looking.

At seven, I heard a knock on the door. As I opened it, Terzi stormed in with Sheikha behind him. I looked at him. He looked back. "We're fucked!" he said.

It turned out the meeting with the Human Rights minister had gone well. He had approved the thirty-two. But afterwards Terzi and Sheikha had gone to pay a courtesy call on Louis Wanza, the director of immigration. Immigration Department people would be doing the final checks on evacuees. No one would be leaving without their go-ahead.

This man, Wanza, had made life miserable for David Derthick and Sheikha on previous evacuations. On one occasion he had held back a plane loaded with evacuees that was already out on the runway ready to take off. We had been assured that Immigration wouldn't present any difficulties this time, but Terzi had thought it wise to pay his respects. "We got in to see him immediately," Terzi said, "and the first thing out of his mouth was, 'Nobody informed me about this. I'm in charge here. I say who leaves and who stays. I'm canceling the flight.'"

The threat was a power play. What Wanza really wanted was to put more of his own people on the flight, but Terzi had refused. "I know this type," Terzi said. "If I said yes, by tomorrow morning he'd have even more people to put on. He's going to wring every last cent he can from this. We're going ahead exactly as we planned. There's nothing else to do."

On their way back from the immigration office, Terzi had called Barry at the US embassy and explained the situation. "I'll see what I can do," Barry told him. He hadn't sounded optimistic. Terzi then tried to call the Human Rights minister—no answer. The minister had approved the list. If he asserted himself, maybe Wanza would be forced to back off. Human Rights had already gotten their additional cases onto the manifest. They had made their money. Now Wanza was trying to squeeze in extra for himself. Maybe that would aggravate the minister enough so he'd actually do something.

Back at the Memling, we sat around worrying. Either Wanza was going to play this to the hilt or he wasn't. We'd either be going or not. Every once in a while Terzi tried the minister again. Still no answer.

Around nine Terzi's phone rang. His face lit up—the minister was on the line. Terzi explained what was happening: he had taken the list to Immigration to get their approval, but Wanza was holding things up, he wouldn't stamp it. Wasn't there something the minister could do? We'd worked together so well. Everybody's needs had been taken care of. Didn't the minister think he could break the logjam here, to make sure we could take off tomorrow with all the people Human Rights had approved?

He'd see, the minister said. Unfortunately, he was leaving in the morning on a state visit to Spain. He'd try to take care of it, but he wouldn't have much time, his flight was early. Still, he'd make a couple of calls. He'd let us know.

That was it. We knew the man wasn't going to do a thing. He had no reason to, no incentive. None of the people he had forced on us were going to come back to him for refunds.

Terzi hung out until eleven. We felt like we were looking into a black hole. None of us had any idea what the next day might bring. Our plans were all set. I'd pick up the buses early, then I'd meet Sheikha at the protection compound. Meanwhile, Terzi would go to Immigration for one last shot. The whole thing looked like it was going to ride on what might happen between him and Wanza.

After Terzi left, Sheikha and I were too wound up to sleep. We sprawled out next to each other on the big sofa, semi-comatose but still on edge, caught between exhaustion and frustration. Jacob Batend was on both of our minds, Jacob and the thirty-two. I couldn't get the images of those stick children out of my head or the haunted faces of their mothers. I kept picturing the two withered, dying infants.

As I got the money envelopes ready for the people we still had to pay off, we went over the agenda and who we'd need to do what: the police for the crowd, the armed guards for the buses, the immigration officials who would do the final checks. When I finished with the money we packed our bags. We wouldn't be coming back to the Memling any time soon.

We finally went off to bed, Sheikha to her room, me to mine. I set two alarms for 5:00 A.M., my cell phone and my travel clock, afraid I might sleep through one of them. Knowing Sheikha, she probably wouldn't get any sleep at all. She was too angry. We were on the verge of getting everybody out, the widows and orphans as well as the 112 we came for. And now the whole thing was hostage to this one money-hungry son of a bitch.

At five, the sky was still pitch black. I made sure Sheikha was up, then grabbed my things and took the elevator down to the lobby. My car was waiting. Neither the driver nor I said a word as we sped through the deserted streets to the City Train transportation depot.

The manager wasn't there, and the assistant manager was someone I hadn't seen before. "Yes, sir, I have your three buses right here." He gave me a big, ingratiating smile. "As you know, the fourth is undergoing repairs."

This was how it worked here, everyone trying to squeeze out a few extra bucks. "We made arrangements," I said. "Your manager and I. I know he's made that clear to you. I want all the buses, four of them. Please. *Now.*" He scuttled off and a few minutes later four buses pulled up. I got on the first and we drove out in convoy, heading for the protection center.

When we arrived, Sheikha and Denis Pirlot, our IOM doctor, were already there. It was 7:00 A.M., four hours till the Cameroon Air's departure time. The armed guards had shown up and were milling around with their AKs, along with Captain Jose and his police squad. But the immigration officials were missing, the ones who needed to do the final checks before anyone could board. It was possible that Wanza was going to stop the whole thing.

I had arranged with our drivers to pick up the immigration officials at their houses. I told them that if necessary they should bang on their doors and get them out of bed. But what if they had been told not to come? Wanza might be angry, but would he put himself at loggerheads with the minister? Beyond that, the United States was funding this mission. Washington's weight was behind it. Everyone knew that.

I paced back and forth like an expectant father, watching the compound gates, thinking *Okay, now! Open up now!* Sheikha flashed me a brief smile. I knew what she was thinking, what she found amusing. How could I possibly expect we were going to keep to a schedule? She didn't say a word, but I could hear her anyway. "We're in Africa, Sasha, in the Congo. Schedule? What's wrong with you? We're on Congo time." Ten minutes passed, then fifteen, then half an hour. Still no Immigration. "What do we do? Any thoughts?" I asked her. "Do?" she said. "There's nothing to do. It's out of our hands. Don't worry so much. They'll be here."

At 8:30 A.M., my phone rang. One of the drivers, I thought, telling me what's going on. But it was Terzi, calling from the Immigration office. I could hardly hear him, his voice was faint through the static. "Sasha . . . very important . . ." I couldn't make it out. What was important? The line went dead—signal lost. I ran to the top of the hill where we had done the registering. The reception had been terrible from day one, but sometimes it was better up there. No luck, no bars.

At 8:45 I asked Captain Jose to begin the personal and baggage inspections. We had to get things started, even if these Immigration people weren't here. The Cameroon Air pilot had told me the airport authorities had given him a departure window. They were being pissy about it too. If we missed the window there might be problems.

The police were looking through people's bags when my phone rang again. Not Terzi this time; it was the Belgian ambassador, looking for Terzi. *Monsieur, c'est tres important. Nous avons un autre . . .* fade out. Thank God. They had another for us to put on the flight. All the coalition partners knew today was evacuation day. I wondered who else might call, what other embassies. None, I hoped.

Over to the side. Sheikha was monitoring the police as they patted people down and searched their things. In the previous evacuations the police had stolen everything they could get their hands on, stripping the refugees of whatever little they had managed to bring with them. Now they were taking birth certificates, school papers, medical records and tearing them up. They were destroying everything that showed citizenship or any other connection to the Congo. "Why are you doing this?" Sheikha was yelling at them. "They're already leaving. It makes no sense!" She was right up in their faces; the woman had absolutely no fear. "The students need their records! People need their medical certificates! Leave them alone!"

"No!" This from the hard-looking cop she was yelling at. "These records are fake! These people are not Congolese."

"If they're not Congolese, what are they? Where is their home? Where is their country?" Sheikha said. "Haven't you done enough? Haven't you humiliated these people enough? They've lost their homes, they've lost their families, and now even their papers? No one will know the date they were born, where they were born, where they went to school. How low can you go?"

"No, no, no! You be quiet! These people are Rwandese!"

"What is wrong with you?" Sheikha was practically beside herself. "They're not Rwandese. They're Congolese! They're from the Congo. This is where they are. This is where they live."

The torn pieces floated to the ground, fragments of names and dates, the last bits of identities, littering the dirt around the pile of bags and battered suitcases.

At 9:00 A.M., the first car arrived with two Immigration people. There were supposed to be four. As they got out of the car I asked, "Where are your colleagues? Where are the other two?" They didn't know. They were two hours late and they didn't know where the others were. And no, they said, there was no way for them to start the processing without the others.

Ten minutes later, another car pulled up with the two others, the one Derthick had nicknamed "Twoface" and the one he called "the Limper." "Twoface," Derthick had told me, "an evil bastard on the take." The Limper, "pretty decent. Possibly even helpful."

As fast as we could we got everybody lined up by order of the bus they'd be going in, one, two, and three. The Immigration people had the lists and photos. They started checking people off and boarding them. Sheikha and I were standing next to Twoface when Jacob Batend came up.

"Not you," said Twoface. "You stand over there."

My heart stopped.

"What do you mean?" Sheikha said. "He's approved. He's on the list!"

"No," said Twoface. "This one's not going. Who's next?"

Sheikha and I looked at each other. This had to have come straight from Wanza. I didn't know what was going through Sheikha's mind, but I was desperately trying to think of what to say, which wasn't helped by the rage building up inside me.

Then Jean Baptiste, the head ICRC person, stepped in front of him, saying quietly, but with a hard edge in his voice, "This man is on our list. Look." He shoved the list under Twoface's nose. "This list is stamped approved by the Minister of Human Rights. This is his seal. Do you see it? This is his signature. Do you see it? Do you have a countermanding order? If you do, show it to me. If not, then you have no right to keep this man here, and you will bear the consequences if you do." Then louder. "Show me your documentation!"

Twoface stared at him. He had nothing. And there in front of him was a minister's seal and signature. You could see him trying to figure out which would be worse for him, disobeying whatever he had heard from Wanza or disobeying a ministerial order in black and white. His bureaucratic mind teetered back and forth. Then he stepped back. Jacob climbed onto the bus.

The boarding continued. The group of thirty-two prison survivors got up from where they were sitting and came toward the third bus. One of the teenage girls was smiling, but most still looked shell-shocked. Barefoot and without luggage, they climbed the bus steps, two mothers holding the small children, the silent boy Daniel with the baby on his back, then the third mother carrying the two dying infants.

As the buses finished loading, I noticed the Interahamwe killer watching from the crowd the police were holding back. I scanned faces for the other killers we knew were there. I had been worried about this since our first day here. Were they planning something? Here, before we left? Or maybe an ambush on the road by some nameless militia group nobody would ever be able to identify?

The crowd of refugees who were not going was pressing against the police line. They had been shouting since the boarding began, but it was as if my hearing had tuned out and now was coming back. People were crying, calling out last-minute pleas. "How can you leave us here? Please don't leave us! Please!" Once I had heard Roméo Dallaire, the Canadian general who had commanded the UN troops in Rwanda during the genocide, describe what it was like to leave people to their fates, to look into their eyes and know you simply cannot help them. It broke his heart, Dallaire said. My heart too, I thought. Mine too. Then I blocked it out.

When everyone was finally on board, I gave Sheikha and Denis Pirlot the manifests for their buses. I was going in the first bus with Captain Jose, Sheikha would be in the second, Pirlot in the third with the thirty-two from the tent. The fourth was empty, my backup, just in case. I had broken down the evacuation list into subsidiary lists of those riding in each bus and made sure the refugees boarded the right buses. "Go through your lists," I told Sheikha and Pirlot. "Make sure everyone with children knows what age they're supposed to be." Then I stepped up into the first bus and all four buses pulled out in a cloud of exhaust. The compound gates closed behind us.

A little way down the road my phone rang. Terzi.

"Sasha?"

"Davide. I'm in the lead bus. We're on our way to the airport."

"Good." I could hear him perfectly, the line clear for a change. "I'm still here with this bastard," he said. "Make sure you don't stop, not for anything. Do you understand? Do not stop! I'll see you at the airport."

As the bus bumped and swayed over the pockmarked road, I moved down the aisle, holding on to the seats, squatting next to the families with children, telling them, "We have too many people for the flight. What we've done is change some ages, because children under two can sit on laps. We've made your four- and three- and two-year-olds into one-year-olds. When you get on the plane, have them sit on your lap. If anyone asks you, you say they're one year old. If anybody gives you any trouble, you tell them to talk to me or Sheikha. We have the list showing the ages. Do you understand? Good."

A half hour later we drove through Ndjili market, the place where Sheikha and Derthick had had a flat tire on one of their evacuations, where they had been a moment away from being overwhelmed by a lynch mob. The market was thronged with midmorning shoppers. I imagined it all happening again, the guards out with their AKs, the mob howling for Tutsi blood. When we passed the market I let out a deep exhale. I hadn't even realized I was holding my breath.

Halfway down the aisle a woman in a frayed red shirt gestured to me. I squatted down beside her. "Are we really getting out of here?" she asked. She was shaking all over. "Yes," I said, "we'll be at the airport soon. We're getting on a plane and flying to Cameroon." Trying to convey a sense of confidence I wasn't exactly feeling. Who knew what was really going to happen when we got to the airport? "Do you know what they did to me?" she said. Her eyes were leaking tears. "Do you know what they did to me in prison?" She didn't have to tell me. I knew. I had heard too many stories already.

At the airport we snaked around the perimeter fence and found the gate opened for us onto the tarmac. I could see the Cameroon Air jet, sitting by itself away from the terminal, the gangway stairs up against the plane's open door. We pulled up fifty yards from the plane, so near, I thought, but still so far. The bus doors opened and I stepped down with Captain Jose and our guards into a little huddle of immigration agents, already waiting. To my right I could see Sheikha and Pirlot getting out of their buses. In front of me, between the bus and the plane, a double row of people were standing in what looked like a receiving line. I saw Barry from the embassy, UNHCR people, ICRC officers, officials from the Ministry of Human Rights, and others I didn't recognize, no doubt from NGOs and other embassies. Congolese soldiers were all over the place. I looked around for Terzi but couldn't find him. Wanza wasn't there either. Maybe they were coming together.

The immigration officials started calling people off the first bus, one family at a time, checking names and photos, just as they had when they boarded back at the protection center. The woman in the tattered red shirt came down. From yards away I could see her trembling as the agent scrutinized her and her picture. She moved past the immigration officer and walked gingerly through the double line of onlookers toward the gangway, as if stepping too fast might bring the wrath of her tormentors down on her before she could escape through the plane's open doorway. Suddenly she faltered. A hand reached out to steady her and she moved on, slow but determined, her eyes fixed on the plane.

As her foot touched the bottom step of the gangway, she stopped and glanced around quickly, as if she was afraid they would pull her back even now. Exactly that had happened last time. Security guards had grabbed a number of people and shunted them off somewhere. Most had ended up back in the protection center, but a few hadn't. The ICRC had pushed to find out what happened to them but learned nothing. They were just gone, vanished. Nobody stopped the woman in red, though. She disappeared into the plane without looking back again.

When I looked up I saw that Terzi had arrived with Wanza. They were standing on the tarmac talking at each other, both of them obviously heated—Terzi, the Italian, gesticulating with his hands. The first bus was almost empty now. I looked for Jacob and found him. He had been put to the back of the line. As he stepped down, he was told to get onto the second bus. Now Sheikha was standing next to me, her eyes, like mine, riveted on Jacob as he moved to the back of bus two. I looked back at Terzi and Wanza. That's what they're waiting for, I thought. For that argument to be over so they'll know what to do with him.

The second bus emptied. They put Jacob in the back of the third bus with the widows and orphans. Sheikha and I watched as the silent boy Daniel stepped down, the baby strapped to his back, the three other children holding hands. Behind them came the mother with the twin infants. She looked dazed, unsure where she was. The process stopped. They were holding them up. Something was going on, but from this distance we couldn't tell what. I took a step toward them, but a soldier with an AK shoved me back. A horrible thought came to me. This woman and her children had been through the worst. They were witnesses. If they left, they could speak out about what they had seen. No, that was crazy. Almost every Tutsi was a witness. What could they possibly want with women and children, especially these women and children?

Minutes passed. What could he be asking her? It was taking forever. They have to let them go, I thought. Rivulets of sweat were running down my back. Finally, at last, the woman began walking, slowly, her twins in her arms, her other children after her. Past the double line of onlookers and onto the plane. A minute later the next death camp families followed them.

I watched the prison group going through the lines and up the stairway to the plane. When I looked back, I saw Jacob staring at me through the bus windows, searching for a sign. I realized Sheikha wasn't at my side. I turned. There she was, walking off toward Terzi and Wanza. She stopped, talked to them for a moment, then she was coming back, shaking her head. She could hardly choke out the words. "Sasha, Wanza isn't going to let him go."

I turned back to Jacob, still staring at me through the bus window. Questioning. *What's happening? Am I getting out of here?* I thought about his wife and children, waiting for him in Cameroon. Terzi was still arguing. Was there anything else to do, I thought, any other leverage? Could I go over there and make some point, twist Wanza's arm somehow, appeal to his humanity? Say something Terzi wasn't saying? It was senseless to even think so. I looked up at Jacob. I shook my head slowly, deliberately. No. No, you are not going. Jacob's head fell to his chest. His shoulders slumped. I couldn't tell if he was crying; it looked as if he might be. As they led him off the bus, Jacob's eyes met Sheikha's, then mine. Then he was gone.

After the last people from bus three had boarded, Sheikha, Pirlot, and I made our way onto the plane. The cabin was steaming. For the last who-knew-how-long the plane had been sitting there with its engines and air conditioning off. The outside temperature was close to a hundred, the humidity nearly the same. Inside the plane was like a sauna.

People were clustered in the aisle around the mother with the twins. Sheikha and I threaded our way through them and looked down. The babies seemed barely alive. One's tongue was hanging out, as if he had lost control of his muscles. Heavy green mucous dribbled from his nostrils. Sheikha grabbed both babies and unswaddled them. I pulled a water bottle out of my bag and moistened their lips. I sprinkled some water on their bodies to cool them. Then we heard the engines whine to life and cool air began coursing through the cabin.

As the engines revved up, Sheikha went through the plane distributing diapers, giving quick lessons on how to use them. We gave out water bottles, settling people down. Almost everyone here was a first-time flier. No one wanted any hysterics, especially the crew. In fact, we wanted as little crew involvement as possible, especially when I saw two of the stewardesses eyeing the large children sitting on their parents' laps. What would we say if the crew made an issue of it? "No, what do you mean? Of course they're one year old. They're just very tall. All these Tutsi people are very tall."

I had imagined this moment, our takeoff. I had pictured a huge cheer resounding through the cabin as the plane left the ground. Maybe I'd get up and shout "We made it!" while a torrent of joy broke loose. I imagined how the refugees would feel. They had gotten out of hell. They were safe and secure. Many of them had family waiting for them in Cameroon with open arms.

As the plane started moving, I turned in my seat. The first person to catch my eye was weeping. Here and there others were too. I knew they were crying for Jacob. He had left his mark on them with his caring and generous spirit. In the months he spent in the protection center he had counseled them and helped take care of them. He was, really, their leader. And now? Taken away from them and left behind to meet what was certain to be a very bad end.

I half stood up and looked around the plane again. Every seat was taken. It was hard not to feel good about that. I looked at the people crying. Then I saw Sheikha sitting next to the death camp mom, each of them cradling a tiny infant. I saw the dozens of other children, many on their parents' laps. I saw the lady in the red shirt, the silent boy and his four charges, the two other death camp mothers with all theirs. I thought of the families in Cameroon, hearing that we had taken off. Good news, they say, can travel like the speed of light.

PART II

THE MORAL
DECISION
PATHWAY

THE CIRCUMSTANCES OF SASHA AND SHEIKHA'S DILEMMA WERE EXTREME, but the situation itself is one we all confront at one time or another. A decision point presents itself. We are motivated by the expectations of others to take a particular action, or perhaps we know that deciding in a certain way will advance our careers, enhance our status, or at least keep us out of danger. And yet, another option is available, one we are reluctant to entertain, which we'd like to dismiss or disregard, one that challenges our innate resistance to taking risks, yet nevertheless calls to something inside us.

In our story, Sasha is not prepared for the challenge that un-expectedly confronts him. Yet something compels him to follow Sheikha into the tent, and what he finds there opens his eyes. Here are the first two principles in the decision-making pathway.

1. **Be prepared.** Be prepared to understand that these decisions come upon us, most often unexpectedly. Sheikha is prepared here, but Sasha is not.

2. **Open your eyes.** Sasha accepts the need to look, and what he finds opens his eyes to the moral challenge in front of him.

For Sasha, "opening his eyes" meant becoming fully alive to the dilemma confronting him. His orders were clear; they came from his boss, whom he trusted. The downside risk of doing something other than what he had been tasked to do was grave.

3. **Confront yourself.** The power of Sheikha's moral certainty forced Sasha to confront himself, to plumb the depths of his personal value system, something he had never previously been called on to do.

4. **Know yourself.** In confronting himself during the course of that long night's debate, Sasha came to recognize that the humanitarian values—that is to say, the altruistic, empathetic, compassionate values—were those that most truly defined who he was. When that night was over, he knew who he was in a way he had not known prior to entering this crucible.

5. **Take courage.** Knowing himself, making his decision on the basis of self-knowledge then required action. It meant dispel-ling fears and taking courage in order to find a solution and implement the decision he and Sheikha had made.

Sasha was truly caught in a crucible, with many lives in the balance. People in other walks of life face decisions that are similarly critical: first responders, triage physicians, soldiers in combat. But these are likewise out of the ordinary. Does the exceptionality of Sasha's situation mean that it has little significance for most of us? We believe the opposite is true. The underlying features of Sasha and Sheikha's decision, and how they arrived at it, are universal.

The stories in Part II are by and about people who have been through their own crucibles, stories that illuminate elements of the critical decision pathway we've defined. The accounts we're presenting in this section are about people from various walks of life, all of whom we have interviewed, most of whom we know well. A distinguished business professor is here; a Navy SEAL; a former US surgeon general; a family doctor; a senior aid agency officer; two CEOs, one a Holocaust survivor, one a technology guru.

Some accounts are longer than others, but we have tried to present all of them so that the contexts of our contributors' decision points are fleshed out and our contributors themselves come across in something approaching full-face portraits. Not all of the narratives illustrate all the principles in our five-step pathway, but each, we think, is powerful in terms of its own focus.

The stories in this section are contextualized with discussions of current research about how morality is a hardwired component of our essential selves. Finally, we address the potential of altruistic or empathetic decision making to spark personal transformations that can, at times, lead to lifetime callings.

FOUR

EMPATHY

Where the Moral Sense Comes From

> *How selfish soever man may be supposed, there*
> *are evidently some principles in his nature,*
> *which interest him in the fortune of others,*
> *and render their happiness necessary to him,*
> *though he derives nothing from it except the*
> *pleasure of seeing it.*
>
> Adam Smith

> *Are we humanitarians or are we not?*
>
> Sheikha Ali

The universality of our five-step pathway is embedded in one of the most widely recognized stories in the entire historical record. Moshe Rabbeinu (Moses Our Teacher), as he is known in Jewish literature, is the iconic leader of the Exodus who gave the Children of Israel—and the rest of the world—the great moral code of the Ten Commandments. We think of him leading the Jews out of slavery, raising his staff and commanding the sea to part, or descending the mountain with the two tablets. He stands in both myth and belief as the great liberator and lawgiver. But in reflecting on the critical moments in Moses's life, it is his vulnerable, human side that bears attention, in particular the experience that changed him from what he was into what he would become.

Moses's defining moment took place on a hot day in the mountains of Midian while he was herding his father-in-law's sheep. There he notices a strange phenomenon, a bush on fire, yet not burning up. "I need to take a look at this," Moses says to himself—the Biblical language is "Let me turn aside to see." When he does turn aside he hears a voice calling him—God's voice, telling him that it is his, Moses's, job to go to Egypt and, number one, persuade the Jews to follow him and number two, persuade Pharaoh to free them from their enslavement.

Moses at this point is a simple shepherd. He has never been anyone's leader, and he is quite sure this is not a job he's up to doing. So he reacts like most of us might if faced with a challenge we don't want, weren't expecting, and can't see ourselves undertaking. He balks. He shies away. "Who am I to do this?" he asks.

When God explains that He will be with him, Moses says, "How can I approach the Israelites? I don't even know Your name so I can convince them You spoke with me." God tells him His name. "They still won't trust me," says Moses. God tries further to persuade Moses. "But I'm a slow speaker," says Moses. "I have a speech impediment." God says He will be with Moses's words, He will instruct him what to say. "Please send someone else," says Moses.

Of course, in the end Moses cannot resist—although that's a questionable point. God can, after all, be argued with, even persuaded. Abraham does it when he argues with God about destroying the wicked city of Sodom, and Moses himself does it later on Mount Sinai when he persuades God not to wipe out the people because of their sin with the golden calf. In any event, here Moses is overawed and takes on the challenge. That is, he opens his eyes, he confronts himself, he accepts that with God's help he will have the ability to see this task through. He takes his courage in hand. And though he does not know it yet, he will be transformed by the experience.

The story is a powerful narrative, one of the most memorable we have. Beneath the action, the Bible lays out what constitutes the defining experience in the life of its most towering figure. The text is Moses's encounter with the Divine. The subtext is the roller coaster of how Moses recognizes and responds to the challenge.

We can discern here the basic elements of our pathway: the recognition, the confrontation, the understanding, the courageous undertaking. In what sense, though, is Moses prepared for this ordeal? In fact, he is emphatic that he is *not* prepared, that he isn't fit. Regardless of his deep anxiety and fear, is there some kind of preparation for this in Moses's past? It's now that we remember why he is in Midian in the first place.

Back when he was an adopted prince in Pharaoh's household, Moses went out to watch how his brother Hebrews were suffering. When he sees an Egyptian beating one of the Jewish slaves, he attacks and kills the Egyptian. Now a wanted murderer, he flees to the safety of the Midian mountains. There he is, resting near a well, when a group of young women come to draw water for their flocks. As he watches, some shepherds approach and begin harassing the girls. Moses confronts the shepherds, drives them off, and rescues their victims.

There is something at work here in Moses's DNA, a strong protective instinct and a courageous personality. He kills the abusive Egyptian. He fights for the defenseless girls. When God calls on him from the burning bush he does not want to face the challenge. He argues, he stalls, he makes excuses. He tries to shift the burden off to someone else, anyone else. But beneath the fear and reluctance there is something in him that is ready to do this. Although he doesn't even overtly recognize it in himself, he is prepared for the challenge facing him.

Moses's story suggests that we all have inside us the potential to face the critical decisions that challenge us, whether or not we recognize it. "I need to take a look at this," Moses says to himself. The exact wording, "Let me turn aside to see," is one of the Old Testament's most telling phrases. What is it, then, that prepares us to take that look, to "turn aside and see" rather than just walk on?

There's no single answer here. Sasha followed Sheikha to the tent where the widows and orphans were, even though his rational mind was screaming at him not to. He didn't have time to reflect on what made him do that, he just did it. Other people in other situations may be more aware that in the depths of their character they have what it takes. "Some qualities were there waiting for life to pull those things out of me," Common Cause founder John Gardner told Warren Bennis. The first step in finding those qualities requires an open set of eyes. You have to be ready, as the Biblical author says, to "turn aside and see."

Jim Post is a prominent business professor at the Boston University School of Management. Born and raised Catholic, he became a leader in the Voice of the Faithful Movement of Catholic laypeople that sprang out of the shocked reaction to the priest sexual abuse scandal. One morning in early January 2002 just before he and his wife, Jeannette, left for their usual attendance at Sunday Mass, Post picked up the *Boston Globe* and saw headlines that propelled him into a state of profound confusion.

The *Globe* article revealed a history of sexual molestation of children by a priest named John Geoghan and, worse, a cover-up by

Boston's archbishop, Cardinal Bernard Law, who had moved Geoghan from one parish assignment to another, enabling him to continue his abuse of children.

Jim and Jeannette were hardly alone in their feelings of shocked disbelief. The greater part of the congregation at St. John the Evangelist in Wellesley, Massachusetts, arrived at church that morning shaken to their roots. As the parish priest led them through the liturgy, questions were percolating throughout the church: "What does this terrible news mean for me and my faith?" and "What am I to do?"

Over the following weeks, an answer evolved that was to jolt the Catholic hierarchy and turn a discussion group of St. John congregants into an international movement for change within the church. Jim Post was among the early leaders of this movement. He ended up serving as president of Voice of the Faithful for five years. Later, reflecting on what opened him to this painful confrontation with the church he loved, he talked about his college experience as one of the factors.

Post attended St. Bonaventure University, a Franciscan institution. The Franciscans have produced some outstanding church intellectuals, but scholarship is not foremost in their mission. Franciscans are known for various core values, among them their devotion to acts of charity and service to others—caring for those in need. "I met men there who devoted themselves to these qualities," says Post. "I saw mature, capable, talented men living out that commitment."

Those men made a permanent impression on Post as an undergraduate. When the older, professorial Jim Post looked in the mirror, that was still very much part of the image that looked back at him. There was nothing heavy-handed about a Franciscan education, but the values embedded in the Franciscan life were there in the background when the sex scandal threw Post—along with so many other believing Catholics—into a crucible that demanded decisions and action.

Joycelyn Elders, former surgeon general of the United States, had her own searing experience that demanded an answer—and that ended by transforming her understanding of who she was, or, as she put it, "what I was about."

Elders was born in 1933 to a sharecropper's family of eight children in southwestern Arkansas. She started working in the fields when she was four years old. With no medical care available for blacks, the first time she ever saw a doctor was at her physical examination as a freshman entering Little Rock's Philander Smith College, to which she had won a scholarship. Elders was a talented, hardworking student and eventually won admission to the University of Arkansas Medical School, where, some years later, she was appointed chief pediatric resident—the first black woman in Arkansas to hold such a position and perhaps the first in the country.

In the years following her residency, Elders emerged as a leading clinician, teacher, and medical researcher. Her husband, Oliver, whom she married while she was in medical school, was the winningest high school basketball coach in Arkansas's basketball-crazy history. They had two children; they lived in a pleasant middle-class neighborhood; they had two good incomes. Elders was becoming widely known for her work on growth hormone and type 1 diabetes. Along with a small group of other pediatricians, she helped establish pediatric endocrinology as a recognized subspecialty.

In 1987, Arkansas governor Bill Clinton asked Elders to take over the state's public health department. It was the last thing she ever would have thought of doing. "I didn't want the job," she said. "It was not the kind of thing you'd give up a professorship for." But how do you say no to a sitting governor, particularly in a small state like Arkansas? She needed a way to turn Clinton down without seeming to turn him down, so she asked him for three things she knew he would never be able to give her: she wanted to retain her university tenure, she wanted a higher salary than what she was making, and she wanted 100 percent political control over the health department—a couple of those requests prohibited under state law. She thought she had gracefully finessed the governor.

Then late one night her phone rang, waking her out of a deep sleep. Clinton was on the line. "You know those things you asked me for?" he said. "Well, I got them. So you'll do it, right?"

"Well," Elders said, "I don't want to be a liar."

"That's real good," said Clinton. "I'll see you in my office on Monday morning."

Shanghaied into a job she did not want, Elders planned to stay for only as long as decency required, then resign and get back to the university. But that was before she began visiting Arkansas's county health clinics. In the poverty-stricken, mostly black Mississippi Delta and in the poverty-stricken, mostly white Ozarks, she saw rates of early teenage pregnancies, low-birth-weight babies, AIDS and other STDs, parasitic infections, cholera, neonatal tetanus, maternal death, and infant mortality that were more like those of a Third World country than a developed one.

All this had me thinking about the life I'd been living for the last twenty-five years and what a tiny scratch I'd been making on the surface. I had just been full of pride about my laboratory and my professorship, but from where I was sitting now the glow didn't look that bright. I used to think that being a professor at the medical school was about the most important thing a person could be in the world. I was very proud of me. Now I began to see that in the total realm of people's needs what I had been doing hadn't made that much of a difference at all.

What hit me like a mule kick was how familiar so much of this was. I had been away from conditions like these for a long time. But I still knew all about them. It was all sitting there in the back of my brain. I just hadn't thought about it forever.

But I hadn't forgotten either. This was all taking me right back to where I came from. I could identify with all of it. I didn't have to think, 'How in God's name do these people survive?' I knew how they survived. They survived the same as we had survived. Ignorant and without help. I'd be telling Oliver the things I was seeing, thinking and telling him, "there but for the grace of God, Oliver. There but for the grace of God."

Elders knew a calling when she heard it. Who better than her to address the drastic health problems brought on by poverty, ignorance, and lack of access to care? "This must be God's mission for me," she said to herself.

Elders's tour through the back reaches of the Arkansas health care morass had opened her eyes. It precipitated a confrontation between the values she was living and values that revealed a deeper meaning of who she was. She went on to become a groundbreaking public health director in Arkansas. Her campaign to cut teenage pregnancy and provide health care for poor children gained national attention and led to her election as president of the Association of State and Territorial Health Officers. When Bill Clinton won the presidency, he named her his first surgeon general, where she continued the battles she had been fighting as a public health director.

"When it comes right down to it," she reflected later, "I don't really think of myself as a model for young black women. If anything, I hope to be some kind of model for disadvantaged young people of all kinds, for kids who don't have the usual models they should be growing up with. I want us to think about those kids as our children. That's what I really want. When you pare away all the excess and get down to the core, that's what I am about."

Had Joycelyn Elders done as she had planned and moved quickly back to her professorship, she would have continued in what was a satisfying career. In fact, she later did go back to her clinic and her research. But if she had not opened her eyes to the lives of those in such desperate need, it is unlikely she would ever have gotten down to the "core" that so truly defined her.

Navy SEAL Lieutenant Commander Eric Greitens's defining moment was not very different from that of Joycelyn Elders. Greitens is one of those people with a résumé that seems surreal. As an undergraduate, he spent time with refugees in Croatia and Rwanda, winning awards for his photojournalism in those places. He then won a Rhodes scholarship to Oxford, where he earned a doctorate in politics. His dissertation was about the most effective ways of protecting refugee children. Strength, he concluded, was as important as compassion, so he became a Navy SEAL and served four tours in Iraq and Afghanistan. His book *The Heart and the Fist* was a best-seller. *Fortune* named him one of the world's fifty greatest leaders. *Time* included him on its list of 100 Most Influential People in the World. All this before he was forty.

In Iraq, one of Greitens's close buddies was killed, someone who had protected him during a suicide attack. Other friends were badly injured. When Greitens returned home, he went to Bethesda Naval Hospital to visit the wounded warriors there. When he asked them what they most wanted after they recovered, the answers were always the same: they wanted to rejoin their units. Their buddies, their service, had given their lives purpose. Lying in the hospital they were thinking about that. What kind of purpose would they have now?

"And what if you can't go back right away?" Greitens asked them. One was thinking of going to college to get a teaching degree. Another said, "Maybe I could go home and be some kind of coach or mentor for young kids." A third wanted to stay at Bethesda to help other wounded Marines recover.

Greitens had seen in his work with refugees that whatever the suffering they had been through, finding a purpose was essential in their struggle to recover from their terrible losses. His insight there was more or less identical with that of psychiatrist Viktor Frankl, who survived Auschwitz and wrote *Man's Search for Meaning*. "What man actually needs is . . . the call of a potential meaning waiting to be fulfilled."

When he visited Bethesda, Greitens was himself unclear about his future. As an Oxford PhD and a Navy SEAL officer, he knew there were money-making opportunities for him in corporate America. But his encounter with the wounded Marines opened his eyes to a different path. What they needed most, he understood, was exactly that "call of a potential meaning waiting to be fulfilled." "Our wounded veterans had lost a lot," he wrote in *The Heart and the Fist*. "Some had lost their eyesight. Some their hearing. Some had lost limbs. All of that they could recover from. If they lost their sense of purpose, however, that would be deadly."

Greitens saw that though there were many organizations helping veterans, none were set up to challenge the wounded to continue their service. He thought that if he could somehow provide stipends and mentors to help train vets to serve again in communities, they would embark on paths toward healing by focusing on new purposes in their lives.

At the time, Greitens was living on an air mattress in any empty apartment. But he had saved a little of his combat pay, and when two friends offered to contribute their disability money, he had enough to establish a nonprofit organization, The Mission Continues, and provide his first "fellowship" for a wounded vet. "I understood these men and women," he wrote, "we had worn the same boots, carried the same rifles." "I knew I could do that," Greitens told us when we interviewed him. "I didn't think anyone else had the mixture of experiences that I had. I felt a sense of obligation. If not me, then who?"

Eric Greitens understood that the challenge he was going to give his fellow veterans was the same as the challenge he was giving himself by starting this new endeavor. And none of it was risk free. Or fear free.

"When you're successful at one thing," he told us, "it's a comforting place to be. If you've been a successful entrepreneur or professor or athlete, you build that into your life, with all the reinforcing mechanisms. People clap. They like you. What this leads to is an unwillingness to take risks, because all those accolades are at stake, and now you risk failure. Fear is a natural reaction, fear that you will be a failure."

The Mission Continues was not a failure. On the contrary, it is an award-winning nonprofit that has helped thousands of wounded veterans reintegrate. But starting it required courage. Greitens had faced other defining moments—SEAL Hell Week, mortal combat—but this was different. This was a calling. "You have to be willing," he told us, "if you want to create a greater future self. You have to put your present self at risk if you want to step beyond the margins of your past experience and become something better."

Confronted with the unexpected, Jim Post, Joycelyn Elders, and Eric Greitens had chosen to open their eyes—"to turn aside and see"—rather than walk away. They had made decisions that were to prove literally life changing. But they hadn't faced their challenges unarmed and unprepared. Moral models had been there for Jim Post. Life experience had been there for Joycelyn Elders, providing her with a reservoir of empathy ready to be tapped. Eric Greitens was used to taking risks; in a sense the willingness to challenge his boundaries had become part of him. Different as they were in their backgrounds, their experiences, and their careers, each was drawn by the same underlying feeling for what was required of them. A moral sense, the sociologist James Q. Wilson argued, is natural to mankind. Post, Elders, and Greitens all seem to make a case for the validity of Wilson's argument.

Sheikha Ali had asked Sasha at the end of their nighttime debate, "Are we humanitarians or are we not?" That had crushed his defenses. In a sense, Post the professor, Elders the physician, and Greitens the SEAL had each asked themselves that same question. And each had answered as Sasha had: Yes, I am. Each had made a decision that humanitarian values—compassion, sympathy, protectiveness, caring for others—were bottom-line principles. Their instincts told them that was the case, and they followed their instincts. They did not know where their decisions would lead, or how they might, in the end, transform them into something different ("better," Greitens said). But the desire to look, the willingness to confront themselves, the courage to act were all in place.

According to Plato, Socrates's favorite question to explore with his interlocutors was about the sacred admonition *gnothi seauton*—"know thyself," the maxim engraved on the forecourt wall of the Oracle of Delphi. The admonition was ancient even in Socrates's day. It was enigmatic, capable of various interpretations, and the interlocutors in the *Protagoras*, the *Crito*, the *Phaedrus*, and elsewhere always came up short in these explorations. Socrates considered that he himself was the wisest of men because at least he knew that he did not know.

Are we any closer today to understanding what it means to know yourself? Can we say anything about it that may be relevant for anyone faced with a critical moral decision? In his classic study *The Moral Sense*, James Q. Wilson marshals evidence for a common moral sensibility deeply embedded in human nature. Does this renowned sociologist's conclusion illuminate something essential about what it might mean to know ourselves?

Wilson's book was published in 1993. Another classic work came out a year later, *Descartes' Error*, by the neuroscientist Antonio Damasio. In this book, Damasio spells out how the mind (with its cognitive functions) has evolved from the body (with its emotional systems) and how they function together through neural networks that connect the mechanisms of feeling with the brain's decision-making centers. "Feelings . . . come first in development and retain a subtle primacy that pervades our mental life. . . . Their influence is immense." That is, our decision-making mechanisms are nested in the evolutionarily older emotional or limbic systems that generate our basic feelings—for example, those that dispose us toward mutual caring and protection of others.

What, then, is the relationship between Wilson's "natural moral sense" and our hardwired emotional capacity?

To answer this question, several contemporary research approaches seem to be converging. One is most prominently represented by the primatologist Frans de Waal. From his lifetime studies of monkeys and apes, de Waal concludes that altruism has deep roots within mammalian families closely related to us. He demonstrates convincingly the altruistic behaviors of our close primate cousins. There is, he argues, "an evolutionary basis of human morality." Moral goodness, says De Waal, is real, concrete, scientifically demonstrable, and interwoven with the essentials of who we are as a species.

De Waal's argument is broadened by Patricia Churchland, a MacArthur Fellowship grant winner and professor of neurophilosophy at the University of California at San Diego. Her books *Neurophilosophy* and *Braintrust* make the case for how the activities of the brain and the concepts of the mind that philosophers discuss, such as morality, are actually one and the same. Conscious experiences, such as moral values, she says, are continuous with the brain and its neural networks. We do not have brains that function in one way and moral selves that make decisions in another. We have, instead, what Churchland calls a mind/brain, in which mental states, such as valuing, and brain states, such as neurological activity, are "interanimated."

Churchland's thesis brings together philosophical concerns and neuroscience research. Her arguments are not easy for laypeople. But the essence of her pioneering work, at least for our purposes, is that our deepest selves include the predisposition for moral action—that is, for altruism and care for our fellows. In order to know ourselves, we think she would say, a requirement would be to know at least this.

Damasio (indirectly), de Waal, Churchland, and even more recently, Donald Pfaff of Rockefeller University, make convincing arguments for the hardwired nature of human morality. Pfaff, in *The Altruistic Brain*, demonstrates the precise neural and hormonal pathways by which altruism manifests itself, positing what he calls ABT, altruistic brain theory.

These thinkers and researchers help us understand the "how" of moral behavior, though not the mysterious process by which the discovery of self impacts individuals' lives and consequently the lives of those they deal with. That is the subject of our next chapters.

FIVE

SELF-KNOWLEDGE

How Self-Knowledge Impacts Leadership and Organizations

Gnothi seauton: Know thyself.
Delphic aphorism

With our thoughts we make the world.
Gautama Buddha, *The Dhammapada*

Manfred Kets de Vries is a distinguished professor of leadership development and organizational change at INSEAD, one of the world's leading business schools. Kets de Vries is known for bringing a psychotherapeutic perspective to his seminars and consulting work with many of the world's largest companies. "It turns out," he says, that CEOs and senior business leaders "don't really want to be exposed to more economic models; they want to think about the direction of their lives."

One primary focus of Kets de Vries's work is finding methods to reorient the excessive narcissism he sees in many business leaders, to move them away from self-centeredness and toward realizing "the complexity and value of other people." For Kets de Vries, authentic leaders are those who embody this sensitivity toward others, which gives them a competitive advantage in building successful organizations. "Authentic leaders are cultural architects, creating a framework for the kind of values that make an organization a great place to work. They introduce a set of meta-values into their organizations—values that transcend the more traditional, generic listing of values found in most organizations . . . The first of these meta-values is a sense of community."

Kets de Vries's thoughts about a sense of community propelling business success can hardly help but bring to mind Fred Smith's FedEx. Smith's insight about putting teams together around mission and purpose derives, as he explains it, from his experience as a Marine officer in Vietnam. Smith has been able to imbue his managers and other employees with a feeling of communal values that bind them more closely to each other than is common in business. These values enhance the idea that they are providing a meaningful service to customers rather than simply fulfilling nine-to-five work demands. Teams work together and count on each other. When individuals are linked together, they are often capable of going beyond what might ordinarily be expected—a Marine tenet embedded in the way FedEx operates. Smith is, in Kets de Vries's term, the cultural architect of his company, the leader who thinks not just of the bottom line but of the ethos of his workplace and understands how one vitalizes the other.

Kets de Vries believes, with Bennis and others, that a triggering event, some crisis or decisive moment, is so often what propels individuals into a transformational experience. With his psychotherapeutic orientation, however, he also believes that people need some kind of intervention to bring out the potential change a crisis can precipitate (*The Leader on the Couch* is the title of one of his most influential books). If you are truly going to know yourself, Kets de Vries says, you need help. His approach is traditional psychotherapy, an in-depth process that enables patients—in this case his business clients and their companies—to access the subconscious motives driving their personal and corporate lives in order to make fundamental changes.

In our work, we've seen something different from that. For Joycelyn Elders, Eric Greitens, Jim Post, and Sasha, the triggering event opened their eyes to values that were intrinsic to them, deep in their DNA, in there, just not yet realized, "waiting for life to pull them out," as John Gardner put it.

The need to grasp hold of who you truly are is a powerhouse of a drive. Once engaged, it is compelling, undeniable, neglected or frustrated only at a person's psychological peril. The deep self has its own dynamic and imposes its own demands. "The most fundamental principle of all," the rabbinic sage Joseph Soloveitchik wrote in his masterwork, *Halakhic Man*, "is that man must create himself." Soloveitchik's contemporary Erich Fromm expressed something equivalent from a psychologist's perspective: "Man's main task in life is to give birth to himself, to become what he potentially is." The self, we think, does not need to be convinced of this through psychoanalysis or other interventions. There is something deeply instinctive and internally driven about the desire to know ourselves.

The urgency of this desire is illuminated in two stories: one from a doctor who risked losing her practice, and one from a Holocaust survivor who became a captain of American industry. In terms of our five principles, they illustrate not just the need to know ourselves but the large measure of courage that endeavor often requires.

Few stories of self-discovery are more dramatic than that of Dr. Rebecca Davis, a transgendered internist with a large practice in a big city suburb. Davis's patients are mostly Catholic. Many are working class, though she and the health care practitioners who work for her provide primary care for wealthier individuals and homeless people as well.

> Even before I started medical school, I knew I wanted to be a family doctor. In school I had always been good at math and science, but I also had a strong desire to help people. In terms of medicine, that meant caring for their physical health, but also for their overall well-being. I wanted to practice medicine like the old-fashioned GPs did. I wanted to provide the whole package. I knew that so often health problems are linked to life problems. Alcoholism, stress, anxiety, drug dependency, diet, smoking, job dissatisfaction, relationship problems—so much of what goes on in people's private lives affects their physical health. I wanted to be the kind of doctor who was comfortable sitting down and talking about these things. I wanted to be as good as I could be at the physiopathology side, but I was equally drawn to the holistic side.

Davis opened her practice in 1988, by herself at first, then as it grew she hired other clinicians. From the beginning it gave her tremendous satisfaction.

> Patients responded to my interest in them. I gave them the opportunity to talk about themselves, which they often did. They talked about intimate things. Their married lives, their children, their jobs. They'd tell me about their teenage child using drugs, or how they hated their dead-end job, or how a

love affair was ruining their marriage. Some of them told me about hiding their homosexuality and the shame they felt.

I didn't necessarily have answers, but I tried to share whatever understanding I did have, along with treating their physical ills that sometimes were a direct consequence of what they were going through. I wasn't just checking off boxes, I was treating the whole person. I tried to focus them on the future so at least they could begin to confront their problems instead of just wallowing in them—as insurmountable as they could seem. I didn't in any way consider myself a therapist, but I thought that sometimes I could get them to take that all-important first step. If I thought they needed psychiatric help or some other kind of specialized attention, I referred them and did my best to follow up.

Ironically, it was exactly those moments of intimacy with her patients that were also Davis's worst moments:

Here my patients were telling me their most intimate problems. They were listening to me while I was urging them to acknowledge and deal with these things that were troubling them so terribly. And here I was, a fake, a sham, a fraud.

Davis felt she was a fraud because she had lived her life to that point as a man. As far as her patients were concerned, they were being treated by a male doctor named Sidney Berko.

I was a fifty-year-old man with a secret so shameful that I had hidden it not just from others but from myself, for essentially my entire life. While I was listening to my patients, another voice was saying to me, "*You're* counseling *them*? You have one of the darkest secrets imaginable. You are not what you seem to be. You are living your life as a lie. You will die never having lived as a whole human being."

Davis had been suffering from gender dysphoria for as long as she could remember, the conviction that although she was born with a male body, she was in fact not male but female. Twelve years after her gender transition to female, she says:

> It's hard for me now to recall that sense of torture that would well up throughout my life—as a child, wishing to be a girl, and then as I got older and older, fearing I would die never having lived the way I felt I was meant to live.

There came a point where she felt she simply had to live her life as the woman she felt herself to be. She had reached the end of her tolerance for self-deception. Davis began hormone treatments and set a date for sexual reassignment surgery.

It was a decision that entailed untold risk. She had successfully covered up her dysphoria. Doing what she was about to do made her shake with fear for what the consequences might be.

> There's just this feeling that people are going to be revolted by this, that they will revile you. I had no idea what might happen to my practice. What would my patients think if the doctor they knew and trusted suddenly emerged as not Dr. Sidney Berko, but as a woman doctor with a woman's name? They had confided in me, but I never had to tell them anything private about myself. The thought of literally thousands of patients knowing something so personal about me was unfathomably painful. How could they ever trust me again? Would they leave in droves? Would I still even have a practice?

In the event, only a few did leave. Almost all were somewhat shocked or at least seriously surprised. But the primary factor was that most were seeing her because they felt that she was a good doctor who was giving them excellent care. And that overrode whatever discomfort they may have had about her change of gender.

Interestingly, the main thing that changed for me was the doctor–patient relationship. From having the sort of shame that made me think I was going to have to leave the practice because I couldn't bear that people would know something so intimate about me, I instead began to think, "Oh, since they know something already really personal about me, I can more easily open aspects of my own experience—if it's germane—to their problems, their situations." So it had a freeing-up effect, where I was no longer the high priest, or priestess, which is so typical in the doctor–patient relationship. I was more equal, on one level, which was always what I had wanted.

When you show caring about another person, you do break some barriers of this hierarchy. Not "How was your vacation? How are the children?" superficial and perfunctory, as it may be for many doctors. It gave me an avenue to bring to bear aspects of my own life—again, if it was appropriate—so the patient would feel that he or she was not alone in their current challenge.

It didn't interfere with the patient's experience of my treating him or her medically. I was still the doctor, the one with the expertise. But for me it was basically a whole new way of seeing the world. Since I'm being true to myself, I'm being true to the idea that all people are created equal. That we really are all connected to one another. Not isolated, not alone, even though we may feel that, most especially when we are hurting or in distress.

There's a part of medicine that is very much about compassion. It's not just about looking at the disease and saying, this is the treatment, this is the plan. Here's the prescription.

Go get your x-ray. Next? There is a big part that's about connecting to the patients' joy and sorrow and potential suffering. Not just the formality, not just fighting disease. It's about treating the human being.

Davis's practice, like all medical practices, was a business. Her ability to take hold of her own identity, to understand it and act on it, affected the way she worked and the impact she made on her patients. It enabled her to realize her aspiration to provide health care that was, at its core, egalitarian and humanistic. Not only was she not forced to close her doors, but her practice thrived.

"There is something about our interconnectedness with the human family," says business consultant Chris Osorio, "We are so interdependent. We need each other. Becoming aware of this has profound implications."

William "Wilo" Ungar lost his young wife, their baby, and his entire extended family in the Holocaust. A technical school instructor in Ukraine, he arrived in the United States in 1946 on one of the first ships carrying Jewish war survivors from Europe. Initially finding work as a machinist in a factory that produced envelope-making equipment, he eventually built his own envelope company, which came to dominate the industry.

Ungar's story of survival is remarkable. He escaped from several concentration camps and closed-off ghettos. He was saved by a Polish student of his, Edward Wawer, who gave Ungar his own identity papers without asking anything in return. Ungar was arrested again and escaped again. For nine months he hid in a coal bin in the basement of an apartment house occupied by Gestapo officers and their families. Finally, when the Red Army arrived in his city, Lvov, he emerged tentatively into the daylight and made his way toward the Polytechnic University, where the Soviet hammer and sickle flag was flying from a high turret.

The university's main building was being used as an army headquarters and hospital. When Ungar came in, a dying man on a stretcher called to him: a young rabbi friend he had not seen for three years and assumed was dead. Rabbi Bartfelt had just come out of hiding too, only to be shot by thugs from the anti-Semitic Polish Underground.

That night Ungar was back in his now-deserted apartment building. His previous experience with the Russians had taught him that if you already lived someplace, there was a good chance you could stay there, but if you waited for them to assign you a place, you could wait forever. That morning he had awakened in a coal bin. Now he took possession of a two-bedroom apartment.

As night fell, he sat at his new desk fiddling with a pen he had found. Years later he told the story to one of this book's authors: "I had sat down intending to write my name on a piece of paper to insert in the nameplate on the apartment door, to claim it for myself. Instead I was overwhelmed by a tidal wave of sorrow. I was almost comatose. My head was flooded with black thoughts."

In his book *Destined to Live*, Ungar gives a complete description of this earthshaking moment.

> My left hand took the little square of paper . . . With the pen I wrote my name, bearing down hard to impress the letters on the surface of the paper. Not "Wilo Ungar," but "Edward Wawer." Tears streamed down my cheeks as I opened the door and inserted it into the bracket.
>
> That night I lay awake. From far away came the tap tap tap of machine gun fire and now and then a muffled explosion.

It sounded as if the Germans were making a fight of it on the outskirts. I hardly cared. I was finished with my suffering. All I wanted to do was forget it, consign it to hell and move on from it. I felt as if this day I had stood at a crossroads. Who needed to live a life like this when some other kind of life was available? Who needed to live with such hatred, from these people who had sucked the milk of anti-Semitism from their mothers' breasts . . . After all, what did I have but this one fragile life, which I had miraculously managed to preserve, not once, but half a dozen times? Why, when it would mean peace and finally a chance for happiness by giving up this unbearable burden, which I hadn't chosen anyway but which had been thrust upon me. My nameplate read "Edward Wawer." My birth certificate read "Edward Wawer." So be it, I thought. From now on I will be Edward Wawer.

At dawn I was still awake. Having made the decision was so simple and, in a way, so right. What could be more logical than for someone in Poland to be a Pole? But instead of a peaceful, dreamless sleep, I was kept awake by what seemed a multitude of voices and images. They crowded in, one after another, among them the cheerful, cracked voice of my grandmother. "Remember, Wolce"—she said this to me every time we visited her in Postulufka. "Remember your grandfather whom you are named after. Remember your good name, Wolce, your *shem tov.*"

That morning Ungar got up from a sleepless bed, took Edward Wawer's name out from his nameplate and replaced it with his own.

Forty-seven years later, Ungar went back to Ukraine to visit the scenes of his childhood and youth and find the places where his extended family had met their fates. He was then seventy-nine years old. In America he had created a second life for himself. He had fallen in love and married. He and his wife had four daughters, all adults now with their own children. He had started a business with three antiquated envelope-making machines and had built it into the biggest envelope producer in the country. In the process he had made a fortune and become well-known for his philanthropy and personal generosity. He was one of the founders of the United States Holocaust Memorial Museum; he built schools in the United States and Israel. He had received numerous business and philanthropic awards.

Now, back in Ukraine he was reliving events whose memory he had tried for years to suppress. At the Belzec death camp, where his young wife and baby died, he walked through the little park the Soviets had created to mark this place where over half a million people had been gassed and turned to bone and ash. A monument there declared what the Germans had done, but neglected to mention that they had done it to Jews. The ground beneath Ungar's feet had a strange brittle quality to it. Before the Red Army arrived in 1943, the Germans had exhumed the remains, re-burned them, and crushed and buried the bones. At Belzec the bone shards of half a million people still permeated the former camp's soil.

At the back of the park Ungar found a bench and sat down, conjuring up the image of his wife and baby as they must have experienced their walk from the railhead to the gas chamber. Edward Wawer was in his mind too.

I thought about Edward Wawer, whose name had saved my life so many times. I thought about that night so long ago when I had wrestled with myself over who I was going to be. A new man insisting on his right to live life free of an intolerable burden of suffering. A new man abandoning the terrible confines of his people's inheritance and his own pain, boldly making his unfettered way into the future. I remembered how fierce that struggle had been inside myself. And I thought, sitting there in Belzec, how puerile such a life would have been.

Remember your *shem tov*, his grandmother had said—your good name. As a youngster studying the Book of Proverbs, Ungar had learned that "A good name is worth more than riches." It had been a lesson repeated again and again by his family. It was almost a family mantra. He had tried hard to live up to it, not just in his personal life but in his business life.

> I'm more and more aware that my success was truly a result of personal principles translated into business terms—business values. How you treat others personally, how you are responsible for many, not just yourself. How money by itself cannot be your guiding star. How we don't live in a zero sum game. You can succeed without hurting your employees and without treating even your adversaries unfairly.

That was what his *shem tov* had meant to him, his own version of knowing himself and acting on that knowledge, an organic outgrowth, as he put it, of characteristics instilled in him by his parents, his faith, and his experience of the Holocaust. For William Ungar, *shem tov* was shorthand for the requirement to live a compassionate, moral-centered life.

Both Rebecca Davis and William Ungar understood the grave risks their decisions entailed. Dr. Davis was putting her hard-won medical practice in danger. She was risking shame and calumny. In embracing his Jewish identity, William Ungar was courting a highly uncertain future. Jews were still being killed on the streets. The German Army might counterattack and sweep up those who had survived in hiding—as it in fact did in several places.

Defining moments almost always carry downsides. They tend to be fraught with risk, which is what makes them momentous in the first place. For both Ungar and Davis, the decisions they made defined their characters and shaped their lives. Moreover, the decisions informed their ongoing work lives; in different ways, the values these decisions clarified infused themselves into their businesses.

Our next two stories bring this last principle into relief. What happens to an organization when a leader brings the lessons he or she has learned into the organizational setting? Leaders, says Ket de Vries, are "cultural architects." Defining moments, says Joseph Badarocco, "can matter as much to the life of an organization as they do to the life and career of a manager." "Managers," he says, "are the ethics teachers of their organizations."

Mohammed Abdiker oversees global emergency responses for the International Organization for Migration, the same organization that sent Sasha and his colleague Sheikha into the Congo on their Tutsi rescue mission. In 2011, Abdiker was in charge of IOM's attempt to extricate thousands of migrant laborers trapped by the fighting between Libya's strongman, Muammar Gaddafi, and rebels seeking to overthrow him. Our second leader is Sam Pitroda. Pitroda is the inventor and technology guru who revolutionized Indian telecommunications and connected a billion people with each other and with the world beyond their villages. He served as a cabinet-level technology advisor to seven Indian prime ministers.

By April 2011, the uprising in Libya against Muammar Gaddafi was entering a crucial phase. Rebels had taken Benghazi and were wresting other regions of the country from loyalist forces. Misrata, Libya's third-largest city, was the scene of a fierce back and forth battle between rebels who had taken the city and the army, which was trying to push them out. Gaddafi's forces were rocketing and shelling the city. The Misrata hospital was overflowing, its ICU unit full of the near dead.

In the midst of the chaos, almost 10,000 migrant workers were huddled at the port, hoping for rescue. The migrants were laborers from various African countries who had been working in Libya's oil facilities and other industries. They had been caught in the middle of the rebellion. Those who were working and living near Libya's borders with Chad, Egypt, or Tunisia were fleeing to those countries. Others were trapped, with no food, no water, no medical attention. The thousands stranded in Misrata were being shelled along with the rest of the city's population. In their encampments by the port's quayside, they were increasingly desperate. NATO had promised protection, but there was no protection from the Grad rockets and 81mm mortar shells. Rescue ships were offshore but were staying out of range. Gaddafi had announced that any ship entering the port would be a target.

At IOM's control center in Geneva, Mohammed Abdiker was receiving information from multiple sources: the UN, NATO command, rebel militia communiqués, monitored broadcasts from Gaddafi's military, messages from NGOs in the area, and, most importantly, from IOM's own team on the ground in Misrata. Ambassadors from the migrants' home countries had been in and out of his office pleading with him to get their people out.

Abdiker had the boats to take the ICU patients and the trapped migrants to safety, but he had been keeping them offshore out of rocket range, hoping the situation would clarify or stabilize so he could make a logical decision. Technically, he wasn't even allowed to go in. Because the port was being bombed, the UN had pulled out. No UN entities were being allowed into the area. IOM wasn't a UN entity, but it was a partner, and the UN was telling IOM to stay out too. NATO was also telling them to keep away. They were going to start bombing the Gaddafi positions around the port. Any ship trying to get in might find itself in the way of NATO operations.

The boat captains and crews were prepared to go in, but they didn't have all the information about the danger. Besides, it wasn't their decision, it was his. He was responsible for their lives and for the ships.

> The migrants were innocent victims. Their lives were at risk, including women and children, because some of them had families with them. Every rocket salvo was killing people. They weren't going to get out if we didn't send in the boats. I didn't want our staff to face this kind of risk. I had to do everything I could to keep our people safe. Besides, nobody was requiring us to go in there. In fact, we were being told not to do it. None of the other organizations with boats were sending them into the port. It seemed way too risky. IOM wasn't going to lose out in any way if we didn't send ours in. Our reputation wasn't going to be hurt. Nobody expected it of us.

The situation was only getting worse. On April 15, at two in the morning, the leader of the IOM ground team called from the port, telling Abdiker the crisis point had been reached. He had to make a decision now.

> I sat alone with it for some time. But this was something the director general had to make a decision on. I called him and explained the situation. He told me, "Go in if you think you'll succeed. Don't go in if you think you won't."

William Swing was the IOM director general, the former US ambassador to the Congo. He understood that Abdiker was the one who had the information, that his was the judgment that needed to prevail. But he was also saying that, whatever the decision, he had Abdiker's back.

Essentially, he was telling me, you make the decision, but I'll give my blessing to whatever you do. But I still knew that if a boat got hit, or if our people were killed, that would be bad for me and for IOM. No matter what, we would be getting in NATO's way, and they weren't going to be happy about that. That could create problems for IOM in the future.

Erik Greitens, the Navy SEAL officer, had experienced risks in his career prior to the defining moment he encountered at Bethesda Naval Hospital. Those experiences had made it easier for him to take the path he did. Mohammed Abdiker was also no stranger to risk.

In my work with IOM I had taken risks before, when I worked in Zimbabwe, for example, even though they didn't have quite the same stake as the risks involved in the Libya evacuation. It was when President Mugabe had forced the white farmers to vacate their farms. In doing this he essentially cut off the food supply to the country and hundreds of thousands started starving. When I took over as IOM's chief of mission in Zimbabwe, the whole NGO community was in the capital, but their hands were tied. They couldn't help those who were starving. When I asked why, they said that Mugabe didn't acknowledge there was a problem, so if any NGO tried to address the problem, this would actually highlight that there *was* a problem. And that NGO would be kicked out of the country.

I said that I was going to try and get food to those in the countryside who were starving. All the other NGO leaders thought it wouldn't work and that I'd get IOM kicked out. But through careful negotiations with the government, and by changing the food bags from US branded bags to neutral bags, I was able to get food to hundreds of thousands of people. In that case it was a choice between my reputation (and IOM's) and trying to help starving people. I learned from that situation that you can succeed even when others don't think it's possible. And that situation helped me to build an understanding that in this line of work you need to take those risks sometimes. So I had experiences before the Libya evacuation that I could draw on. They helped me to make that decision. It was about not worrying about my own career or even about IOM's reputation. It was about keeping those who need help in the forefront of my mind.

Abdiker decided to send in a ship. It would deliver medical supplies for the hospital and take as many people out as it could without overloading. As the ship moved into the port, mortar shells were falling. Just before it arrived, another rocket salvo hit the area, killing five people. Smoke from explosions and fires billowed into the sky.

The boat docked safely but needed several hours to unload and load. The operation was precarious from beginning to end. Back in Geneva, Abdiker told his wife, "This is the most terrible decision I've ever made. I've put the life of the IOM staff, the boat master, everyone, at risk."

The first boat made it out safely. After that he sent in others. "Every time a boat went into the dock was the worst moment for me." But, almost miraculously, none of the boats were hit. Almost 10,000 migrants were taken out of Misrata. In the end, IOM was able to evacuate almost 250,000 migrants and refugees from the Libyan war zone.

After it was done, I said to myself, so much is possible in the humanitarian field. We are just afraid to take the risk. We often don't try to see if we can save people's lives. Maybe all the restrictions we put on ourselves limit us. In the humanitarian system, we may feel we can't do what's possible because it's too dangerous.

During the fighting in Sri Lanka between the government and the Tamil Tigers, 40,000 Tamils were killed more or less in front of the international organizations. I saw individuals in positions of authority unwilling to take action because they were afraid they would be kicked out of the country. But people need to speak their mind and protect the most vulnerable. They are worried about risking their salaries, their jobs, so they don't stick their necks out. Sticking your neck out is a radical way of thinking, but it's necessary in this line of work. After Misrata that's how I felt. I felt that way before Misrata, too, but after it this way of thinking was confirmed in me. Misrata was a life-changing decision for me. And it also changed the organization.

IOM shifted how it operates because of this success. We created an emergency fund to do these kinds of things. A number of governments, starting with those whose people we evacuated, gave to this fund. We started doing more emergency work because of this success. I personally felt more of an ability to lead emergency evacuations. When the Ebola crisis hit in West Africa, we were among the first responders. There were very few doctors on the ground in West Africa. IOM found a way to recruit and send in thousands of doctors very quickly. Governments essentially gave us all the funding we needed to get in there. Our ability to respond quickly and decisively was rooted in part in that Libya evacuation's success.

Kets de Vries talks about the powerful connection between the personal values of an organization's leaders and the way the organization itself seeks to achieve its objectives. "This linkage comes about," he writes, "because we are what we think. In other words, all that we are arises within our thoughts; with our thoughts we make our world."

Mohammed Abdiker's defining moment during the Libyan war was life changing for him. And because he was one of IOM's leaders, it helped reshape the way the organization understood and pursued its mission, deepening its commitment and significantly broadening its perspective.

The story of the telecommunication revolution Satyanarayan "Sam" Pitroda brought about in India paints an especially clear-cut, not to say dramatic, picture of a leader infusing his values into his business.

Sam Pitroda was born in 1942 in a small backwater village in Orissa, one of India's poorest states. His father was a blacksmith who went into the lumber business, making enough money to send Pitroda to a Gandhian boarding school, then high school in the Gujarati city of Baroda. After high school, Pitroda attended the Maharaja Sayajirao University, graduating in 1964 with an honors degree in physics.

Pitroda could have stayed on at the university as a junior faculty member, but America beckoned. A graduate degree from an American institution would ensure his future, and the United States was the place where the best physics was happening. When Pitroda heard that one of his close friends had been accepted into a PhD program at the Illinois Institute of Technology, he decided to go with him.

In the late fall of 1965, Pitroda and his friend, Bhupen Trevidi, left India by steamer, embarking through Mumbai's monumental Gateway of India. They both felt they were beginning the adventure of their lives. But as they stood at the rail watching the Gateway slip below the horizon, Pitroda was overcome by a feeling of loss.

Suddenly it seemed to me as if I had lost my entire life. Somehow the earth had moved. Everything was gone, back there below the horizon, my family, my friends, my connections, my roots . . . all of it lost. We were alone on a vast, empty sea. I felt a surge of emotion. Tears welled up, but I blinked them back.

The feeling didn't leave. Later that night he stared out at the blackness.

For the first time in my life I found myself thinking about India itself, my home place, the place I loved and had always taken so completely for granted. India contained so much, so many languages and cultures and peoples, all mixed together. India had mystics and snake charmers, gods and goddesses. It had music and dancing, its own colors and sounds, smells, the taste of spices. We had been served such a bland dinner that evening in the ship's dining room. Whoever thought of spices, until suddenly there were no spices? I had never valued them. I had never valued any of it.

I had left that world, for good, it seemed to me then . . . . not just my parents and sisters and brothers, but my country, my land. It was gone, vanished back there in the blackness. I felt a love for India like nothing I had ever felt before. I felt so heartsick that for a moment I wondered if I would survive. I swore that I would never forget. I would cherish my memories. No matter what happened, I would keep them with me forever.

It was an experience whose poignancy Pitroda would recall vividly fifty-plus years later when he told us this story. This was not a defining moment in terms of imposing the need to make a moral decision, but it was without any doubt a crucible. It defined for Pitroda his indelible bond with the country of his birth, which was to have profound significance for the course of his later life.

That night at the ship's railing confirmed for Pitroda who he was and who he would always be. But he was about to encounter in the United States an astonishingly different set of values from those he had grown up with, which would exert their own formative influence on him.

At the Illinois Institute of Technology, Pitroda found a style of teaching that had little to do with what he was used to back in India.

One of my professors was a Dr. Messenger, who taught a signal analysis course I took that first semester. In one class, he was trying to solve a particularly complex equation. The problem was on the board and Dr. Messenger was trying various possible solutions but having no luck. "This is a tough problem," he said. "I can't seem to solve it." His eyes picked out one of the students. "John!" he said. "John's smart. Maybe John can solve it. Get up, John."

So John got up and went to the board. Dr. Messenger sat down in John's chair, looking at the board while John started working the problem.

I was watching the board too, but I was also looking at Dr. Messenger. I was wondering: What kind of professor is this who says I can't do it, but my student can do it? And then sits down in the student's chair to watch?

I'd more or less just arrived from India, where this scene would never take place in a million years. And, of course, then John solved the problem.

"See!" Dr. Messenger said. He was ecstatic. "See! I told you he could solve this thing! I knew he could do it!"

What was going on here? What kind of teacher was this? An Indian professor would never admit in class that he couldn't solve a problem. And the last thing he would ever do would be to give credit to a student who could solve it. My respect for Messenger rocketed straight up. He admits he can't solve it? He loves the student who can do it? I thought, what a great guy! And he wasn't faking it. He was genuinely happy that he couldn't do it, but his student did it. Unbelievable!

Not all the IIT professors were like Messenger, but to someone accustomed to the strict hierarchy of Indian institutions, even a modicum of egalitarianism in student–professor relationships came as a revelation.

Not long after Pitroda graduated he got a job at GTE, which assigned him to a small group working on digital telephone switching. Scientists at Bell Labs had discovered how to digitize voice signals, which was revolutionizing telecommunications. Digitized voice signals needed to be transmitted through digitized switches, which was what Pitroda's team was working on.

At GTE, Pitroda discovered he had a talent for this technology. By the time he was thirty he was a senior scientist with an international reputation. A few years later he was tapped to run a startup switching company, which pioneered major breakthroughs in the industry. A few years after that he sold the company to Rockwell International, becoming both a multimillionaire and vice president for technology for the giant conglomerate.

At meetings of top managers and CEOs of Rockwell's various businesses, Pitroda saw an extension of the same kind of egalitarianism he had experienced at IIT. At these meetings the participants, each one the head of a major business, paid no attention to who stood where on the corporate ladder.

After the general meeting, we'd break up into small groups. As soon as we did that somebody said, "Okay, you take notes, you're the chairman, you get the pizza, you make the coffee." And people just did it. Somebody at random divided up the tasks and everybody did what they were supposed to.

That happened at all the big meetings. These men were
the chief corporate executives, and nobody ever complained
that "I made coffee three times" or "I ordered the food last
time." There was no hierarchy. I thought, could this ever happen in India? Maybe it didn't happen at other big American
companies either; I didn't know. But in India, with its culture
of deference and hierarchy? Never.

On a trip to Delhi, Pitroda took a suite at one of the city's most
exclusive hotels. When he tried to call his wife back in Chicago to tell
her he had arrived safely, the call didn't go through. He tried a second
time; it still didn't. The hotel sent someone up, but he wasn't successful either.

The next morning, Pitroda looked out the window and saw a
large funeral procession passing the hotel. But the procession seemed
a little odd. The crowd was carrying a funeral litter, but there was no
body on it. Instead, it was piled high with dead phones.

Telephones, my specialty, were being paraded through the
streets. When I asked the doorman what was going on, he
said, "Oh, it's just the phone problem. It takes ten years to
get one, and then the damned things never work. People get
upset." The next day the newspaper had a big article about
the dead phone demonstration.

After that, Pitroda couldn't get India's phone situation out of his
head. It became an obsession.

With a lot of arrogance and even more ignorance, I thought,
who better to fix it than me? This is something I need to do.
I am going to fix it!

As a top-level Rockwell executive at the cutting edge of the telecom revolution, Pitroda's career in the United States was essentially

without limits. But though he had been living in America for almost twenty years and had become an American citizen, in his heart he was no less Indian than he had been the day he left Mumbai as a student and watched the Gateway of India slide below the horizon.

Moreover, Pitroda was a low-caste village Indian, with an indelible memory of the backwardness and poverty of rural Indian life. Like Joycelyn Elders when she took on the public health director's job, his roots called to him. India, with almost a billion people, had only two million telephones, all owned by either companies or the wealthy. (At that time there was a phone for each person in the United States, about 180 million.) The country's 600,000 villages were home to 90 percent of India's population, and they had virtually no communication with the world beyond themselves. In that sense India's villages were medieval enclaves, with impoverished, subsistence economies that had no possibility for growth. Pitroda could see the economic and social revolution that would take place if he could devise a way of providing rural farmers, small merchants, and villagers generally with access to the wider world.

Mahatma Gandhi had been revered in Pitroda's family. Pitroda had gone to a Gandhian school. He had imbibed Gandhian values of love and affection for others and concern for those at the bottom of the economic ladder. His own identity was wrapped up with that of his country. Now, he thought, it was the time to do something for India, in particular for India's poor.

As Pitroda saw it, bringing telecommunication to rural India could help lift tens of millions out of poverty. It would enable small businesspeople to connect with suppliers and customers outside the village confines. It would enable farmers to get information on crops, weather, agricultural developments, and how to expand their markets.

Here was a historical opportunity for me to make a dent. I knew I had to do that. I didn't understand the consequences, that it would require a huge amount of sacrifice on the part of my family. For my children, my wife, for our financial security. But it was something I needed to do.

Pitroda spent the next three years traveling back and forth between India and America, studying India's phone system in depth, developing plans for how to approach the problem, and meeting with people who might help him advance his agenda.

Throughout the world, telecom always started in the cities, where private and business customers were most densely clustered. Pitroda planned to start in the villages, not in urban centers. That was going to require specialized equipment and a breakthrough approach. It was going to mean building a task-oriented business of engineers, fabricators, and suppliers that would operate differently from India's typically hierarchical, sclerotic, bureaucratic companies. When he was finally able to present his plan to Prime Minister Indira Gandhi and she gave him her blessing, he launched the Center for the Development of Telematics, or C-DOT, a completely new kind of business on the Indian scene.

Pitroda brought with him to this venture the egalitarian values he had absorbed in America, ideas about employees taking significant responsibility for their work, about creating incentives for personal and creative growth, about working in teams where leadership was based on expertise rather than hidebound notions of rank. In the digital switching company he sold to Rockwell, he had utilized management techniques that later became popular in Silicon Valley and elsewhere: flat management, nonhierarchical management, open system management. He incorporated these techniques, so contrary to Indian custom, at C-DOT. He hired women, integrating the workplace, unheard of at the time. He hired only young engineers, right out of school. Older people, he believed, were too conditioned to the habits of deference and subservience that characterized the stultifying atmosphere of Indian businesses generally.

In the process of seeding telecom through India's rural villages, C-DOT generated unlooked-for consequences. First and foremost, the company provided a home for Indian graduate engineers, some of the world's best. Prior to C-DOT and the indigenous manufacturing environment C-DOT created, young engineers typically left India for jobs in the US and Europe. After C-DOT, technology opportunities in India burgeoned. It was the beginning of the Indian high-tech revolution.

Through C-DOT, Sam Pitroda himself changed. "It made me see things in many dimensions that I had never seen before," he says. "In economic dimensions, but also in human dimensions." From C-DOT he went on to create and run India's Technology Missions, its National Knowledge Commission, and the National Innovation Council, institutions that have gone a long way toward modernizing the subcontinent.

That simple decision—that he was called to fix India's telephones so that the countryside poor might better prosper—eventually transformed him from a talented technocrat into someone with the confidence and scope to attack issues far larger than the important but narrow expertise he began with. It's a testament to man's potential for development, as well as a demonstration of where a simple moral decision might lead. Pitroda, like most of our other storytellers, first "turned aside to see."

SIX

CALLING
How Crises Lead to Callings

*Every man and woman is born into this world
to do something unique. What is it that you
were born to do?*

Benjamin Mays

A crisis both calls you and empowers you.

Jim Post

Benjamin Elijah Mays was one of the fathers of the Civil Rights struggle. Though he never had the same kind of national recognition as Martin Luther King Jr., James Farmer, or some of the other public faces of the struggle, he was very near the heart of the movement.

Mays grew up on the outskirts of the tiny South Carolina town of Ninety-Six. One of eight children in a sharecropping family, he evinced a drive for education that eventually led him from the cotton fields to Bates College in Maine, where he graduated Phi Beta

Kappa, and then to the University of Chicago, where he earned a PhD in religion and philosophy. Mays was an ordained Baptist minister, a college professor, and dean at Howard University. In 1940, he was appointed president of Atlanta's Morehouse College, a traditional black school that under his leadership became a highly regarded liberal arts institution. "Mays's character and values defined Morehouse," says former Secretary of Health and Human Services Louis Wade Sullivan, a Morehouse graduate. "He inspired a crucial generation of black leaders."

Mays exerted a powerful influence on Andrew Young, Julian Bond, and Maynard Jackson, among other famous and less famous Morehouse alumni. Martin Luther King was his student and protégé; King revered Mays as his "intellectual father," his "spiritual mentor."

For twenty years Mays was a moral force at Morehouse. Every Tuesday morning the entire college met for chapel. Most often Mays himself was the speaker, and his oratory was, by all accounts, extraordinary. He had a ringing voice and a knack for the pithy, memorable phrase. "The tragedy of life," he told his listeners, "doesn't lie in not reaching your goals. The tragedy of life lies in not having goals to reach. Every man and woman is born into this world to do something unique. What is it that *you* were born to do?"

"We listened to that voice and those words," says Sullivan, "and took them to heart. What were *my* goals? What was it that made *me* unique?"

When Jim Post, past president of Voice of the Faithful, talks about the Church crisis that changed his life, he describes the sense of calling that critical event gave him. "A crisis like that," he says, "both calls you and empowers you. You're called to it because there's a moral need, an issue that cries out for attention. And you're empowered to do it because you find you can bring something useful to that discussion, that issue. You find your distinctive competence."

Responding to a crisis, hearing a call, does something beyond revealing an individual's moral core—who he or she is at the deepest level. To "know yourself" is one step in the pathway we've been describing. The next step is "take courage." As Post puts it, "You have to take hold of that responsibility and do something with it."

We mentioned earlier that once you have tapped into your own set of primary values, you will likely understand what the right course of action is for you. That's true in terms of the particular dilemma that challenges you. But moral decisions often have consequences that go far beyond the immediate occasion. We've seen how they enable individuals to inject values into their organizations and businesses. It's also the case that they draw out a person's latent abilities in often unexpected ways. They set people off on different paths in new directions, and new directions almost invariably lead to the development of capabilities that have lain fallow, dormant, unrecognized, and untapped. You find what Post calls your "distinctive competence" or in Benjamin Mays's words, that which "you were born to do."

The poet Robert Frost evokes something of this in his beautiful poem "The Road Not Taken."

> *Two roads diverged in a wood, and I—*
> *I took the one less traveled by,*
> *And that has made all the difference.*

But what does developing a "distinctive competence" actually mean? How does it work out in real life? This is the personal transformation side of the critical decision paradigm.

In one way or another, each of our storytellers is a model here. Their lives illuminate the truly vast potential that making hard, empathetic decisions can unlock, none more so than Sam Pitroda's.

Before he found his calling, Pitroda was a telecom engineer. He built his company, C-DOT, because he felt called to find a way to connect India's billion people with each other. He brought telephones to rural India because that was the way he believed he could best help alleviate the chronic poverty and backwardness of village life.

Building C-DOT, though, dramatically expanded his thinking about what he could do for his country—more specifically, what technology could do. C-DOT gave him an understanding of the political, media, and financial dimensions of working in India. He was at heart a technologist; now he began to consider how technology could be used to bring change to other major segments of Indian life that were mired in stagnation and hopelessness.

Indira Gandhi had given him his first go-ahead. After her assassination in 1984, her son, Rajiv Gandhi, was elected to succeed her. The new prime minister and Pitroda were the same age. They had both been educated outside India, and Gandhi himself had a strong interest in technology. The two men hit it off and quickly developed a close working relationship. Gandhi's backing empowered Pitroda to bring his aspirations to life. With C-DOT well under way, Pitroda turned his attention to creating a massive public and private effort to help address some of the country's most acute problems.

Together with Gandhi, I decided the effort should concentrate on five sectors: rural drinking water, literacy, immunization, edible oils, and telecommunications. Later we added a sixth: dairy production. We would call these the Technology Missions. I would come on as advisor to the prime minister for the Missions. My overall objective would be to mobilize technology to benefit the people, in particular rural people, in the sectors we had identified. In addressing these five, later six, areas I was going to attempt to integrate technological interventions with government efforts, private industry, and volunteer resources.

My job would be to coordinate the ministries and energize the work. I would keep everyone involved focused on goals and timelines. I'd operate independently and bring in new methods of management. These functions were just down my alley. I wasn't a specialist in any of the mission areas other than telecom, but I could be the catalyst for all of them.

The Technology Missions were like nothing India had ever seen. They brought about sweeping changes. A large percentage of Indian villages did not have clean water sources. The Technology Missions focused on 100,000 of these villages. Under Pitroda's direction, the Missions built water treatment facilities and testing labs. Satellite imagery identified potential new water sources. "In these places," he says, "we were able to insure thirty gallons of potable water per day for each person and forty gallons of water for cattle."

The lack of childhood immunization was another huge problem. India had the highest number of polio victims in the world. Even though polio vaccines had been around for several decades, India's record on vaccinations was abysmal. Here the Technology Missions intervened with the medical community, which had spent years arguing whether India should adopt the injectable Salk vaccine or the oral Sabin vaccine, with the result that little progress had been made and tens of millions of Indian parents lived in fear for their children.

Pitroda forced the immunology specialists to reach a consensus. In effect, he herded the country's seventy top experts into a room and told them not to come out until they had made a decision, which turned out to be for the Sabin oral vaccine. But the oral vaccine was made from attenuated live virus, which meant it had to be kept cold during transportation and storage, which in turn meant that so-called "cold chain" refrigeration facilities had to be established throughout the subcontinent. Pitroda called together the relevant industrialists and mobilized them to put cold chain equipment in place.

This by itself was a prodigious effort; then came the immunization campaigns themselves. The effort advanced slowly but at a steady pace. In 1988, India had the world's highest number of polio infections. In 2013, twenty-five years after Pitroda's intervention, India was declared polio free.

The other Mission efforts—literacy, edible oils, dairy, and telecom—brought about similar transformations. Two years into the Missions' literacy campaign, the organization was awarded UNESCO's coveted Noma Literacy Prize. Instead of importing edible oils, India became a major exporter. After Pitroda recruited to the Missions his colleague, the engineer and social entrepreneur Verghese Kurien, India became the world's largest dairy exporter.

Contemplating all this, Pitroda thought, "What a romantic thing to do. What a fulfilling thing to do. To make a difference on education, health, telecom, water, immunization for so many. I didn't know what the future might hold, but for the moment at least, I had found the right outlet for whatever compulsions were driving me—my need to fix things, my intolerance for political and bureaucratic dysfunction, my dreams for a more progressive, more humane India."

Very simply, Pitroda had found his "distinctive competence."

He was hardly finished, though. Thinking about how technology could be brought to bear on India's myriad problems led him to consider that technology was, in essence, only a subspecies of knowledge. How then to mobilize knowledge in general for social advancement and poverty alleviation?

I started out thinking about university reforms. But universities were only one part of the picture. Vocational education was equally important. We didn't just need professionals, we needed skilled people in the trades and services. And we needed to excel. Aside from the top five percent of the universities, the quality of Indian education was simply not good. Also, there had to be equity. The poorest of the poor had to be able to get to the best schools, or at least to good schools. We needed expansion and excellence, but just as important, we needed equity and inclusiveness.

Thinking about all this—growth, education, inclusiveness—I began to understand that in order to accomplish these things on a countrywide scale, we needed to create a countrywide platform, and that platform was knowledge.

I did some searching, and I found that nobody had put together a big national platform on knowledge—no country. The world was moving fast toward transforming itself into a global knowledge community, but no nation had looked at the challenge in a comprehensive way. The next question, then, was: What would a comprehensive knowledge platform look like?

The proposal Pitroda put forward included building fiber optic systems to connect all of India's educational institutions, then building an open access system for all government records, a complete public information infrastructure available to everyone. The proposal was approved in 2005 and the National Knowledge Commission was established. "I was coming to grips," says Pitroda, "with the next phase of India's technology and knowledge revolution. In particular I was now thinking more comprehensively about the India I thought we needed to build."

Here, he believed, innovation plays the key role. If the United States was the most innovation-oriented and innovation-driven country in the world, India was down near the bottom. There were two prongs to changing that situation. One was to figure out how to inject an innovation mindset into a tradition-bound culture. The second was how to bring about innovation focused on the needs of those at the bottom of the economic pyramid—"inclusive innovation."

To meet these goals, Pitroda established India's National Innovation Council, which then created state, sectorial, and city innovation councils, all of which began generating ideas and programs to get old and young schoolchildren involved in innovation. Pitroda himself concentrated on bringing innovative procedures into a dozen central cluster industries.

> Our initial idea on the Innovation Council was to create a psychology primed to innovate. Our job, as I saw it, was to light the fire. India is vast. Its people are resistant to change. But we are making serious inroads.
>
> For us, inclusive innovation is the key. I want to go into these areas where there's a craftsperson, someone making pottery or jewelry or painted tiles, and see how I can improve his livelihood with technology, to increase his income, or her income, because some crafts are traditionally female. The rich man is doing it anyhow. He's globally competitive, selling for export. But often he's exactly the person who's keeping the traditional worker poor, because he's making the margin on the traditional person or small manufacturer's product. Meanwhile the scientists and technologists are working for the rich and nobody's paying attention to the poor.
>
> My intention is to make inclusive innovation a global enterprise, to help lift up those in poverty worldwide. The goal here is to implant the innovative mindset into cultures where this way of creative thinking has never taken hold.

In that regard my own fundamental beliefs centered on democracy, globalization, free market economy, and privatization. But the enabler here, in my view, was democracy. The democratic ethos, its values, its mores, its procedures, its spiritual characteristics, allow for the fulfillment of what it means to be human—to a far greater extent than any other political system. And the essence of democracy, also in my view, is that it recognizes the humanity of each person, which includes empowering all people as full participants in the national community. This is another way of saying that democracy is inclusive. I am a firm believer in democracy, and I am a firm believer in inclusiveness. They are two parts of a whole.

Inclusiveness means that I cannot worry simply about my own well-being, I have to worry about my neighbor's well-being also. In the last two decades, India has done an immense job of raising the standard of living for several hundred million people, but we still have almost 200 million surviving on the edge of subsistence—the largest number of poor in the world. As I saw it, the task of public information and innovation was to bring those at the bottom out of subsistence and into a level of well-being.

One can only wonder what would have happened had not Pitroda made that original, empathy-driven decision, had he not taken that road. "*And I,*" Frost wrote, "*I took the one less traveled by/And that has made all the difference.*"

You're called to it because there's a moral need,
an issue that cries out for attention.
And you're empowered to do it.

Jim Post

Jim Post had been a prominent voice in the business academic community for years before the priest sexual abuse scandal blew up and abruptly "cried out for attention." The John F. Smith Jr. Professor of Management at Boston University's School of Management, he had authored books and articles on corporate governance, accountability, and business ethics. Although Post was born and raised Catholic, he had never considered his Catholicism to be the most essential part of who he was. He and his wife, Jeannette, were regular churchgoers, but beyond that he considered himself what he called "a couch potato Catholic." He never imagined that he and Jeannette would one day find themselves in a church basement in shocked discussion with fellow parishioners about an issue that struck to the very heart of their church and their faith. "I had no idea," he says, "that I was about to step into a new world."

The first meeting in the basement of St. John the Evangelist was billed as a "listening session." Post was engaged, all the participants were, but it didn't occur to him that he would do much more than listen. He did have a few words to say, though, and at the following meeting he took more of a speaking role. As the size of the meetings grew and the discussions became more focused on what actions to take, Post became more visible and better known to the people showing up, now not just from St. John's but from surrounding parishes as well.

Post's fellow parishioner, James Muller, assumed the leadership role in those meetings, which eventually led to the establishment of a formal organization called Voice of the Faithful. Muller came to the leadership role naturally. A Massachusetts General Hospital cardiologist, he headed a research group at the world-renowned Harvard Medical School teaching institution. He also cofounded International Physicians for the Prevention of Nuclear War, and he, along with the other co-founders, received the Nobel Peace Prize for 1985.

It was Muller's vision of what needed to be done that initially mobilized the concerned parishioners into what was fast becoming an articulate and forceful lay entity. As the first Voice of the Faithful president, Muller provided the initial vision. After six months he stepped down from the leadership role, and Post was elected to succeed him.

As president, Post presided over the continuing growth of Voice of the Faithful. Though he was its leader, the group included people who had a far deeper understanding of Catholic Church history, doctrine, and spirituality than he did. It also included extremely accomplished people from a variety of fields: scientists, social scientists, physicians, attorneys. His wife, Jeannette, was a neurologist who was the network director of the VA New England Healthcare System. "I came to the conclusion," Post says, "that my distinctive competence in those settings was to be able to get other people to contribute, to bring their knowledge out. I wasn't the expert at the table. I was the facilitator."

Voice of the Faithful was carving out a radical identity for itself as a lay group challenging the ingrained secrecy that cloaked the Catholic Church hierarchy. They were protesting the abuse scandal, but far more significantly, they were challenging the very structure of a 2,000-year-old entity with a billion adherents worldwide. People asked Post how he thought his little group could actually make any difference in the face of the Church's immense power. The conservative Catholic media attacked them relentlessly. Bishops in various dioceses prohibited Voice of the Faithful groups from meeting on Church property. Voice of the Faithful members faced a concerted effort to portray them as destructive renegades operating outside the bounds of Church law.

Often it seemed to Voice of the Faithful members that the work was too hard and they weren't getting anywhere. "There's a wonderful saying from St. Francis," Post told us.

It came from a time when some of his followers were discouraged by the difficulties of their work. 'First do what's necessary,' Francis told them. 'Then do what's possible. Soon you'll find you are doing the impossible.'

That saying just steamed in from somewhere during some of my darker moments. That was exactly the kind of guidance I needed. Yes, let's do what's necessary. Someone needs to speak out for the survivors of abuse. Someone needs to be a voice for the voiceless. That's something we can do, and that's something our little group felt it was necessary to do, our moral obligation. Then we could think about what's possible, bringing sunlight into the Church. 'Sunlight,' as Justice Louis Brandeis said, 'is the best disinfectant.'

If you had asked me in 2000 or 1999 what it means to be a Catholic, I'm sure I would've given you a fairly simplistic answer about following the guidance of the scriptures and commandments and so forth. But certainly in 2002 and thereafter I had a much more developed view of what it meant to be a Catholic. The positive role of Catholic citizenship, not just complying with rules and laws and so forth, but to take hold of that responsibility and do something with it.

As the scandal enlarged and became ever more inflamed, Post became an increasingly visible spokesman for the group, which was now demanding the resignation of Boston's Cardinal Bernard Law. This was the challenge that exponentially expanded the group's public exposure. A lay group demanding the resignation of one of the princes of the Church drew media attention all over the country.

Interestingly, Jeannette and other women in Voice of the Faithful were perhaps quicker than some of the men to conclude that Law had to go. Jeannette says:

I knew that because I was a woman in the Catholic Church my voice was not one that would fall on open ears. But a lot of us in the formation of Voice of the Faithful were women who came to the front and said, "It's time for *us* to give voice."

One of the things that pushed us was hearing from those who were abused. That was very difficult. Those were powerful meetings, and they were packed. Absolutely powerful. Hundreds of people from our parish, from Our Lady Help of Christians. No matter where we met.

Law's position was always the Church first; it didn't matter. But it did matter. And if this were my child, it would have mattered even more. I don't know if my being a woman was important, but for those of us around the table who were women, a universal comment was "As a mother you would never tolerate this kind of behavior. If you knew about it you would do something about it." And how often did we hear stories about mothers going to the parish priests to talk about the associate who might be doing this sort of stuff? And they would hear, "I'll take care of it." And then they'd move somebody from one parish to the next. As a woman . . . of course you bring that to the table.

Jeannette's convictions pushed Jim, reminiscent to a certain degree of the way Sheikha Ali pushed Sasha. Jeannette was a mother, and she was also the network director for the VA New England Healthcare System, an organization of 10,000 people. Thinking about it years later, Jim said, "If she said this was a situation we would have no tolerance for, that we would have to remove those people—how could you ignore that testimony?"

On December 13, 2002, Cardinal Bernard Law resigned as archbishop of Boston. It was a signal event in what proved to be the ongoing life of Voice of the Faithful. Post says:

I don't think any of the founders had believed where we would be in one year from when we started. The growth, the development, the visibility, was beyond our comprehension. Certainly, for me personally, it was a journey that was very unexpected. I knew that by agreeing to become president I was agreeing to be a voice that was going to speak for the organization. But I didn't expect the kind of public visibility and the impact that followed.

I think one of the things that really changed over that period of time was that I realized whatever I said publicly had a profound impact. It was going to be quoted. Some people would applaud it, some people would attack it . . . Clearly I was operating at a level that I had not previously operated at. One thing I knew was that I had really become the spokesperson. Not just for the organization, but, more than that, for the issues.

After spending close to five years as president, and all the experiences that that involved, there's no doubt that I'm a different person than I was in January 2002. No question.

Some people believe that our time on earth is really just a matter of accident, of what experiences we have and who we know and that there's no plan to it. A lot of my Catholic friends think there's some larger purpose to our lives and they probably differ about how seriously they take the idea of God's hand leading us in one direction or another. My economics friends talk about the invisible hand of the market. I don't know about that . . . [I do] step back and wonder and reflect on what would have been different if I hadn't gotten up and said something on that first day.

Jim Post describes how taking action can propel you into a leadership role.

> A moral need both calls you and empowers you. You become visible. Your opinion counts in ways it previously had not. You find yourself becoming influential, something different from what you were before. You think differently. Your intellectual and emotional settings get rearranged, and your sense of yourself.

That was certainly Joycelyn Elders's experience as Arkansas's director of public health; it was Eric Greitens's experience as head of The Mission Continues. That was Sasha's experience as well, as executive director of RefugePoint, the NGO he founded that was precipitated by the rescue mission he and Sheikha Ali carried out in the Congo. Sasha says:

> That was a seminal experience. It opened my eyes to people who were off the radar, who were not attended to by the humanitarian system. As a refugee worker I had found what I was supposed to be doing. But then, starting with the Congo situation, I realized that there were groups of people that were overlooked. Everywhere I went I found those people.
>
> In the Kakuma refugee camp, I was working with Sudan's Lost Boys, but I found there were also Lost Girls. The girls shared the same story as the boys but were simply not on the resettlement lists. The boys were all living together in their own sections of the camp. You could identify them easily. But the girls were hidden in the general refugee camp community, often with families who were selling them off as brides.

In Nairobi, I met a large group of HIV-positive refugees. The women had been raped in the camps or at some other point in the violence they were fleeing. Now they were ostracized by their communities and had fled to Nairobi with their families. There they were living in the most abject squalor, undocumented, without medical care, ineligible for resettlement to the US, which, at that point, had prohibitions against HIV-positive individuals.

In one place after another, I saw people who fell outside, whose lives were in danger. There were the Gatumba massacre survivors, Congolese Tutsis who had fled the Congo to a UN "safe haven" camp in Burundi, but who were followed and massacred there by extremist militias. The survivors were in hiding. They had no help. The humanitarian system failed them.

I felt a need to do what I could for these people. In Nairobi, Sheikha and I became lightning rods for many Tutsis fleeing in the region. They had heard what happened in the Congo, so they started showing up, many of them young teenagers who were lost and had no idea what to do.

After that Congo experience, I found that I was completely reoriented toward all these people who had fallen off the grid. This was my calling—to attend to these people. They were the most vulnerable; they were the ones who didn't have anybody else. It brought to the fore my need to take action to address their situations.

Afterward I felt as if I had something to say. I can't recall that I had this urge or need to give speeches or write much on refugee issues before. But after the Congo I had something to say.

When I give speeches now, I'm nervous, but what centers me is that beforehand I think about those people we took care of, who were off the grid, the widows and orphans and others. It's quite simple. I think, I'm just a voice for them, because most of them do not have a voice. That's the role I want to play in the world to inspire others to get involved with them. I'm not worried about what I'm going to say. I just feel like, this is my role. I can be a spokesperson, a person speaking for others.

We've entitled this book *From Crisis to Calling* because often defining moments do present themselves as crises, sometimes as large dilemmas involving life and death, more often on a smaller scale but crises nonetheless. We've seen that facing these dilemmas changes people. Crises are defining situations. They shape the way we regard ourselves. They have the potential to change us in unanticipated ways.

Changes can be purely personal. You discover more about your sense of what is right—that's a window into yourself that you didn't previously have. But personal changes can go much further than that. Dilemmas require decisions; decisions require actions. And actions based on moral decisions are rarely one-off. They become part of our personal repertoires; their meaning stays with us. Sometimes the required actions reach deep. They generate a full investment of the self—that is to say, they constitute a calling. When that happens, it not only opens us up to *who* we are but to *what* we are. What our distinctive competence is, what we are uniquely suited to do.

This is what Benjamin Mays's oratory did at Morehouse College. He was essentially asking his students—Martin Luther King Jr., Julian Bond, and all the others—Who are you? Define yourself. And once you've done that, do something with that definition. In other words, find your calling.

We use the word "calling" to mean exactly that: we hear a call from some powerful source that more or less forces us to pursue certain kinds of actions. Not infrequently, when we are invested in this way we naturally begin to collect others around us who are similarly motivated or have a predilection to be similarly motivated. Jim Post saw himself as a spokesperson for the issues. So did Sasha when he founded RefugePoint and Eric Greitens when he founded The Mission Continues. Their success came, and still comes, because opening their eyes to a moral challenge led step by step to self-knowledge, then to action, then to a calling. This is the pathway we have tried to elucidate here.

We couched this book initially in terms of leadership, and how leaders who have a firm grip on their own values are able to infuse their businesses or organizations with moral principle—to become, as Joseph Badaracco put it, "the ethics teachers of their organizations." And it is true that business life by its very nature tends to be a particularly instructive moral theater, pitting the drive for profit against the more empathetic, humane, and communal values incumbent on businesses as the public enterprises they are.

At the same time, it is crystal clear that the kinds of defining moments we've been discussing apply equally to those in other walks of life. They are universal. At some point in our lives significant moral dilemmas confront each of us—in our families, our schools, our social circles, our religious or political lives. In each case, these dilemmas provide opportunities for self-knowledge, for growth, and even for transformation. These situations might pull us in uncomfortable or unfamiliar directions, but if we are open to that, if we come to these dilemmas with an awareness that they are opportunities to be embraced, then we open up our potential to understand ourselves as moral persons.

We have looked briefly at research that shows how morality is hard-wired into our neural networks, interweaving our emotional response systems with our cognitive functions. Morality—compassionate fellow feeling—also seems incontrovertibly to have an evolutionary basis in terms of the adaptive traits of our species. Biology, as Frans de Waal says, sheds light on our human society.

Studies are now appearing in the field of identity research that complement, and perhaps will eventually complete, what we know from the neuroscientists and animal behaviorists. In the search for what makes us essentially human, memory has always drawn the most attention. It is memory that gives us a continuous narrative of ourselves. Mental characteristics have been a candidate as well; each of us, after all, has a distinctive way of thinking. The theory that our dispositions are central to our identities has also figured into such hypotheses—our idiosyncratic likes and dislikes. But these, says Duke University psychologist Nina Strohminger, appear not to be primary after all. The self, she and her colleagues conclude, "is not so much the sum of cognitive faculties as it is an expression of moral sensibility; remove its foothold on that world, and watch the person disappear with it." That is to say, the most essential element in self-identity is neither intelligence, memory, or disposition. It is morality.

We are, at the very bottom of our identities, moral beings. When everything is said and done, that is the measure we accord our lives. It is how we most deeply recognize ourselves, and it is how others recognize us as well. We hope that the stories we have recounted here illuminate something of the pathway that can lead you to becoming the individual you most truly are—if only you first open your eyes.

A FINAL WORD

At the end of their long night's debate, Sheikha Ali asked Sasha, "Are we humanitarians or are we not?" That was the question that crushed Sasha's final defenses. Before it, his boss's orders, the logic of the situation, his assessment of the risk, all crumbled. "Are we humanitarians?" It was a question one refugee worker asked another in the midst of a crisis. But the question applies to anyone who has to make a decision that affects his or her fellow humans. Are we humanitarians? Or are we not?

Most of those who tell their stories in this book didn't think of their decisions in those terms; they responded to an instinct. Sasha followed Sheikha down to the tent though he didn't know why; he just felt he had to. Joycelyn Elders needed to respond to what she saw in Arkansas's health clinics. Eric Greitens felt the same about the wounded Marines in the Bethesda Naval Hospital. Even Sam Pitroda, the telecom guru, who might not have even thought he was making a moral decision; he just knew that India needed phones. And something told him that it was the rural, impoverished Indians who needed them most.

If we look at the research, we can make an educated guess about what it was that drove them. Antonio Damasio tells us about the deep

intertwining of emotion and reason. Donald Pfaff traces the biology
of empathy, Frans de Waal the evolution of altruism. Pfaff wrote of
"how plausible our built-in kindness actually is, how scientifically
reasonable it can be to rely on the idea that we are wired from infancy
to 'do the right thing.'" *From Crisis to Calling* is not a guide to decision making. Sensible, careful decisions can be and are made on the
basis of compelling factors other than empathy. At times both sides
of a decision can be both right and compassionate. But all our stories
suggest that the humanitarian values are important to consult when
making a decision because they are fundamental to our character, our
psyches. We may have good reason for taking some other path, but
we need to be aware that compassion and empathy are a large part of
what we are made of. We ignore that truth at the peril of reinforcing a
lesser, shallower sense of our own self-worth.

We have argued here for the importance of being aware of the potentially defining moments in our lives and embracing them, "turning
aside to see." It's that initial awareness that opens us to the potential
embedded in our empathetic selves. One of Warren Bennis's main
themes is that leaders "are richly endowed with empathy." That's not
the be-all and end-all of leadership, but, after years of close attention,
Bennis concluded that empathy was an essential need of great leaders as they build their organizations and communities. We would say
this is true not only for great leaders, but for anyone confronting life's
hard choices.

Many writers and thinkers have pointed out that the moral
sense—empathy, compassion, altruism—is almost always at war with
other perceived necessities, as it is with other instincts and desires
we harbor inside ourselves. But even unacknowledged or relegated,
it persists; it is there, available, with all its potential transformative
power. "Mankind's moral sense," writes the great sociologist James Q.

Wilson, "is not a strong beacon light, radiating outward to illuminate in sharp outline all that it touches. It is, rather, a small candle flame, casting vague and multiple shadows, flickering and sputtering in the strong winds of power and passion, greed and ideology. But brought close to the heart and cupped in one's hands, it dispels the darkness and warms the soul."

WHERE ARE THEY NOW?

After the Rescue Operation
by
Sasha Chanoff

Jacob Batend

Our arrival in the refugee camp in Cameroon was both joyous and terrible. The reunions of family members—people who hadn't known if their spouses or children would make it out—were like nothing I'd ever seen. But then there was Jacob's wife. With her two children standing nearby, she broke down and fell into Sheikha's arms, completely overwhelmed that we didn't have Jacob with us.

For some time we had no information about Jacob. Then we heard: he was still alive. Congolese soldiers had tried to bring him to a prison where he would have been executed, but the International Committee for the Red Cross representative intervened and made sure he was returned to the safe haven. Six months later, miraculously, he managed to get out to Rwanda. Our understanding was that many people in his community had figured out how to pull the right levers to get him out. I traveled to Rwanda to meet him, and David Derthick and I discussed the situation with the US embassy, which agreed to expedite his resettlement to the United States. He reunited with his wife and children there shortly after I last saw him.

The Thirty-Two Widows and Orphans

I spent time in Cameroon working with this group, and Sheikha accompanied many of them when they traveled to the United States. We have gotten to know them and watched them as they've gone to school, to college, become American citizens, married, and rebuilt their lives.

The twins survived and are (at this writing) in high school. Daniel, the boy who didn't talk, started running track at his high school. He attended college on a track scholarship and was named a cross-country All American. He went on to become a motivational speaker and successful college track coach, earning a master's degree in psychology.

David Derthick

David Derthick received IOM's highest humanitarian award for orchestrating the Congo Tutsis-at-Risk evacuation. He went on to become advisor to Ambassador William Swing, IOM's director general, and, subsequently, to other major chief of mission appointments. At this writing, he is IOM chief of mission in South Sudan overseeing emergency operations across that country.

Sheikha Ali

My colleague Sheikha Ali rose quickly in the ranks of IOM. As an emergency official, she has undertaken operations in Nepal, South Africa, and other countries around the world.

A NOTE ON SOURCES

Our contributors' stories come from interviews and published autobiographies, all used with permission. Most of the autobiographies were written in collaboration with David Chanoff. Full accounts of our contributors' lives can be found in the following books:

Dr. Joycelyn Elders and David Chanoff, *Joycelyn Elders, M.D.: From Sharecropper's Daughter to Surgeon General of the United States of America* (New York: William Morrow, 1996).

Eric Greitens, *The Heart and the Fist: The Education of a Humanitarian, the Making of a Navy SEAL* (New York: Houghton Mifflin Harcourt, 2011).

Sam Pitroda with David Chanoff, *Dreaming Big: My Journey to Connect India* (Gurgaon, India: Penguin Books India, 2015).

William Ungar with David Chanoff, *Destined to Live* (Lanham, MD: University Press of America, 2000).

"Jacob Batend" and "Rebecca Davis," appear under pseudonyms at their request. "Louis Wanza" (the Congo immigration chief) is also a pseudonym.

Additional Sources

Joseph L. Badaracco Jr., *Defining Moments: When Managers Must Choose Between Right and Right* (Boston: Harvard Business School Press, 1997).

Warren G. Bennis, *Geeks and Geezers: How Era, Values, and Defining Moments Shape Leaders* (Boston: Harvard Business School Publishing, 2002).

Bennis, *On Becoming a Leader* (New York: Basic Books, 2003, revised edition).

Antonio R. Damasio, *Decartes' Error* (New York: G.P. Putnum's Sons, 1994).

Frans de Waal, *Primates and Philosophers: How Morality Evolved* (Princeton, NJ: Princeton University Press, 2006).

Viktor E. Frankl, *Man's Search for Meaning* (Boston: Beacon Press, 1st English edition, 1959).

Erich Fromm, *Man for Himself: An Inquiry into the Psychology of Ethics* (New York: Holt, Rinehart and Winston, 1947).

Bill George, *True North: Discover Your Authentic Leadership* (San Francisco: Jossey-Bass, 2007).

Manfred Kets de Vries, *The Leader on the Couch: A Clinical Approach to Changing People and Organizations* (Chichester, UK: John Wiley & Sons, 2006).

Art Kleiner, "The Thought Leader Interview: Manfred F.R. Kets de Vries," *strategy+business* 59 (2010).

Donald W. Pfaff, *The Altruistic Brain: How We Are Naturally Good* (New York: Oxford University Press, 2015).

Adam Smith, *The Theory of Moral Sentiments*, 1759.

Joseph Soloveitchik, *Halakhic Man* (Philadelphia: Jewish Publication Society of America, 1983).

Nina Strohminger and Shaun Nichols, "The Essential Moral Self," *Cognition* 141 (2014).

Louis W. Sullivan, *Breaking Ground: My Life in Medicine* (Athens, GA: University of Georgia Press, 2014).

James Q. Wilson, *The Moral Sense* (New York: Free Press, 1993).

ACKNOWLEDGMENTS

We first want to extend our deep appreciation to the contributors who have made this book possible by allowing us to use their stories. These include James Post, the John F. Smith, Jr. Professor of Management at the Boston University Questrom School of Business; Dr. Jeannette Post, former director, VA New England Health Care Network; Dr. Joycelyn Elders, former United States Surgeon General and professor emerita at the University of Arkansas School of Medicine; Eric Greitens, former Navy SEAL and founder of The Mission Continues; Mohammed Abdiker, director of operations and emergencies, the International Organization for Migration; Dr. "Rebecca Davis," whose name we have changed here at her request, but she knows who she is and how grateful we are to her; "Jacob Batend," whose name we have also changed at his request and who exemplified leadership under the most difficult circumstances; Sam Pitroda, former advisor with Cabinet Ministerial rank to two prime ministers of India on telecom, technology, and public information infrastructure and innovations. Kenneth Freeman, Allen Questrom Professor and dean of Boston University's Questrom School of Business, gave us important advice, as did Carolyn Monaco of Monaco Associates. We would also like to thank our editor at Berrett-Koehler, Neal Maillet, whose help was invaluable in developing the idea for this book. Marni Chanoff's insight and ability to cut through to the essentials has kept us on the rails at critical moments.

The Congo rescue mission helped lead to the creation of RefugePoint, whose purpose is to find solutions for the plight of the world's most at-risk refugees. Sasha has been fortunate in finding in RefugePoint's supporters a community that not only cares deeply, but that has provided the wisdom and resources that have allowed RefugePoint to thrive and contributed to developing the ideas that underlie *From Crisis to Calling*. Among these, we want to express special gratitude to Arthur Dantchik for his warmth and friendship and for always being at the other end of the phone; to Barrie Landry for her creativity, friendship, support, and advice; to Wendy Ettinger for being the root of so much good in the world; to Bill Mayer, Beth Floor, and Stephanie Dodson for their thoughtful feedback, support, and friendship; to Sherman Teichman at the Tufts University Institute for Global Leadership for his friendship and mentoring over so many years; to Rick Wayne for his inspired leadership; and to Jessica Houssain for her own inspired leadership and daily engagement.

Our thanks go also to Anne Marie Burgoyne for her warm friendship and Aristotelian-like advice, so significant to us especially in RefugePoint's formative years; to Monica Winsor for her support and counsel; and to Josh Mailman for his engagement.

Charles Bronfman and Rita Bronfman are friends whose enthusiasm and commitment have been essential not only to RefugePoint, but to a large number of other endeavors dedicated to humanitarianism. They play a global role in furthering mankind's efforts to create decent and just societies. Their associates, Jill Collier Indyk and Jeff Solomon, have given generously of their practical wisdom and guidance. Sasha is indebted as well to Ellen Bronfman Hauptman, Andrew Hauptman, Zach and Lila Hauptman, Stephen Bronfman, and Claudine Blondin Bronfman for the warm welcome they have given him. The entire Charles Bronfman Prize extended family remains essential both in terms of inspiration and collegiality: Jim Wolfensohn and Elaine Wolfensohn, Justice Rosalie Silberman Abella, Amitai Ziv, Dan Meridor, and Rachel Levin. We would not be here without you. Tory Dietel Hopps has been an essential friend and advisor of many years. Bill Draper, Robin Richards Donohoe, and the entire Draper

Richards Kaplan Foundation team, past and present, have provided ongoing encouragement and stimulating advice, especially Rob Kaplan, Jenny Shilling Stein, Christy Chin, Tom Fry, and Brendan Cullen. Eddie Stern, Stephanie Rein, and Ben, Avery, and Ezra Stern have been models of inspired family engagement with refugees.

No one has been more dedicated to alleviating the plight of refugees than Kitty Dukakis, and she and former governor Michael Dukakis have given RefugePoint the benefit of their unique passion and endless energy. Many others have played significant roles in RefugePoint's development, and our debt to each of them is substantial. Dan Draper, Lorna Brett, and Désirée Younge for their commitment and engagement, and all those at Goodwin Procter who have lent their time and talent. Diane Currier for on-call advice at any time. Julian Hayward for his dedication and care. Lekha Singh for her generosity and enthusiasm. George Lehner for his friendship and creativity. The Gleitsman International Activist Award team and, in particular, Casey Otis-Cote for her ongoing input and dedication, Ambassador Swanee Hunt for her thoughtfulness, and David Gergen, Patti Bellinger, Max Bazerman, and Mike Leveriza for their support and encouragement. Echoing Green, which believed in RefugePoint in the earliest days and has always been there, and in particular Cheryl Dorsey and Lara Galinsky. Henry J. Leir, and the Leir Charitable Foundations, Margot Gibis, and Arthur Hoffman for their belief from the very start. The Mulago Foundation and Kevin Starr and Laura Hattendorf for their support and many stimulating questions. Sam Morgan, Nina Gene, and Jasmine Social Investments for their vital support and care. Ashoka and, in particular, Hanae Baruchel and Amy Clark for helping to bring a unique community together. The incredible team at The Moth and in particular Sasha's storytelling guru Meg Bowles for her ongoing wisdom. Ray Chambers for his support, and Patti Chambers and the MCJ Amelior

Foundation. Karen Ansara for her inspiration and leadership. Emily Nielson Jones for leadership and commitment to girls and women, and Deb Veth and the Imago Dei Fund. The steering committee for New England International Donors for the inspiring and supportive community they've built. Susan Sarandon for being there from the beginning. Isabel Allende and Lori Barra for their support and love. Deb Newmyer, Bobby Newmyer, and Sofi Newmyer for their friendship and support. Dave Eggers for his engagement, starting back with the Lost Boys story. Jeff Walker for his wisdom and guidance. Jennifer McCrae and the Exponential Fundraising inaugural class for the inspiration they have provided. The White House World Refugee Day Champions of Change team for their dedication to refugee affairs.

Among the very many who have shown uncommon care, interest, and support for refugees and RefugePoint, our thanks go out to Marcy Gringlas, Joel Greenberg, Sarah Gauger, Oliver Stanton, Jim Greenbaum, Christopher Quinn, Jonathan Bush, Eddie Roche, Chris Osorio, Chuck Slaughter and the Horace W. Goldsmith Foundation, Allan and Shelley Holt, Lisa Walker, Bob Forrester, Bob Patricelli, Kelly Giordiano, and the Newman's Own Foundation. Alessandro d'Ansembourg, Marianne Gimon and the Flora Family Foundation. Steve Killelea, Peder Pedersen, Camilla Shippa and the Charitable Foundation. Ross and Janice Goodman. Judd Apatow and the Apatow-Mann Family Foundation. Anna and Dean Backer and Goldman Sachs Gives, Kyra and Jean Montagu, Sue and Bernie Pucker, Nancy Farese, Mary Ann Stein and the Moriah Fund, Marz Attar and Manijeh Marvastian, Karen Jacobsen, Joan Platt, Carl and Suzie Byers, Melissa and Tom DiTosto, Adam and Jules Janovic, Chris Siege, John Hammock. The Selah Leadership Network for a place of inspiration, EJ Jacobs, Amy Towers, and the Nduna Foundation, Mike and Sara Henry, Amy Herskovitz, Susan Lowenberg and Joyce Newstat, Evan and Jessica McDaniel, Rob Stewart, Damia Cavallari and

Transit Authority Figures, Ken Pruitt and Teresa Doksum Pruitt, Dan Lennon and Stacey Heen Lennon, Steve Roslonek and Steve Songs, Alex Bartlett, Judd and Jackie Tomaselli, Emily and Bob Morrison, Karen Kehela Sherwood, Molly Smith, Abby Shuman, Victor Syrmis, Rebecca Wright and Michael McDonald, Darian Swig, Amy Rao, Joslyn Barnes, Danny Glover, Fred Zeidman, Catherine Keener, Dylan Leiner, Kelly Ryan, Chris Jorgensen, Jamie Levitt, Marcia Mossack, Allison Carmen, Lori Campbell, Roswitha Mueller, Karen Duffy, Anne DeCossey, Kristina Kinsman Maynard, Rich Leimsider, Henok Mehari and Meda Kisivuli, Pamela Hartigan, Amy Toensing, Kyle Peterson, Rik Kranenberg, David Campbell, Christopher Trost, Auli and Kenn Batts, Matt Forti, Sarah Holewinski, and Ambassador Samantha Power.

The team that makes up RefugePoint, past and present, has brought exceptional skills, creativity, and selflessness to bear on some of the world's gravest and most intractable challenges. They have provided hope and the opportunity to reconstitute lives, a service that needs to be noted but can never be adequately acknowledged.

Last, but really first, we want to thank the Chanoff clan, which keeps us going in more ways than we could ever either count or mention: Rachel, Matt, Lisa, Olli, Molly, Lexy Zissu, Eli, Wolf, Yael, Talia, Aili, Lyyli, Lailah, and Hayden, and, above all, to our wives, Marni and Lissu.

INDEX

Italic page number 10 refers to the map.

ABOUT THE AUTHORS

 **Sasha Chanoff** has worked for over two decades in refugee rescue, relief, and resettlement operations. He is the founder and executive director of RefugePoint, an organization that finds lasting solutions for the world's most at-risk refugees. He has consulted with the UN Refugee Agency and worked for the International Organization for Migration across Africa and the Jewish Vocational Service in Boston.

Sasha's work has been featured on *60 Minutes,* in the *New York Times Magazine,* and on National Public Radio, among other media outlets. He is a White House Champion of Change and a recipient of the Charles Bronfman Prize for humanitarian work and the Harvard Center for Public Leadership Gleitsman International Activist Award. He has received social entrepreneur fellowships from the Draper Richards Kaplan Foundation, Echoing Green, and Ashoka.

Sasha serves on the steering committee of New England International Donors, is a human rights advisor to the Leir Charitable Foundations, and advises The Good Lie Fund, the philanthropic affiliate of *The Good Lie,* a Warner Brothers feature film about the resettlement of the Sudanese Lost Boys.

Sasha holds a BA from Wesleyan University and an MA in humanitarian assistance from the Tufts University Fletcher School of Law and Diplomacy and the Friedman School of Nutrition Science and Policy.

© Heidi Laikari

David Chanoff received his BA from Johns Hopkins University and his PhD in English and American literature from Brandeis University. He has written on current affairs, foreign policy, education, refugee issues, literary history, and other subjects for such publications as the *New York Times Magazine*, *Wall Street Journal*, *New Republic*, *Washington Quarterly*, *American Journal of Education*, *New York Review of Books*, *Washington Post*, and *American Scholar*. He is a featured writer in the *Washington Post*'s anthology *The Writing Life* and his work appears in the current (12th) edition of *The Norton Reader: An Anthology of Nonfiction*. His academic affiliations have been with Tufts University, Harvard, Boston College, and Brandeis in fields as varied as psychology, English language and literature, and anthropology. His eighteen books include collaborations with former surgeon general Dr. Joycelyn Elders, health care disparities expert Dr. Augustus White, former Israeli prime minister Ariel Sharon, former chairman of the Joint Chiefs of Staff Admiral William Crowe, and former secretary of health and human services Dr. Louis Sullivan. His latest book is a collaboration with longtime Ohio representative Louis Stokes.

David is a founding board member of South Sudanese Enrichment for Families, a nonprofit that supports the Sudanese Lost Boy and Lost Girl resettlement communities in Massachusetts. He was an original board member of RefugePoint, of which his son Sasha is founder and executive director.

Berrett–Koehler
Publishers

Berrett-Koehler is an independent publisher dedicated to an ambitious mission: *connecting people and ideas to create a world that works for all*.

We believe that to truly create a better world, action is needed at all levels—individual, organizational, and societal. At the individual level, our publications help people align their lives with their values and with their aspirations for a better world. At the organizational level, our publications promote progressive leadership and management practices, socially responsible approaches to business, and humane and effective organizations. At the societal level, our publications advance social and economic justice, shared prosperity, sustainability, and new solutions to national and global issues.

A major theme of our publications is "Opening Up New Space." Berrett-Koehler titles challenge conventional thinking, introduce new ideas, and foster positive change. Their common quest is changing the underlying beliefs, mindsets, institutions, and structures that keep generating the same cycles of problems, no matter who our leaders are or what improvement programs we adopt.

We strive to practice what we preach—to operate our publishing company in line with the ideas in our books. At the core of our approach is stewardship, which we define as a deep sense of responsibility to administer the company for the benefit of all of our "stakeholder" groups: authors, customers, employees, investors, service providers, and the communities and environment around us.

We are grateful to the thousands of readers, authors, and other friends of the company who consider themselves to be part of the "BK Community." We hope that you, too, will join us in our mission.

A BK Currents Book

This book is part of our BK Currents series. BK Currents books advance social and economic justice by exploring the critical intersections between business and society. Offering a unique combination of thoughtful analysis and progressive alternatives, BK Currents books promote positive change at the national and global levels. To find out more, visit **www.bkconnection .com**.

Berrett–Koehler
Publishers

Connecting people and ideas
to create a world that works for all

Dear Reader,

Thank you for picking up this book and joining our worldwide community
of Berrett-Koehler readers. We share ideas that bring positive change into
people's lives, organizations, and society.

To welcome you, we'd like to offer you a free e-book. You can pick from
among twelve of our bestselling books by entering the promotional code
BKP92E here: http://www.bkconnection.com/welcome.

When you claim your free e-book, we'll also send you a copy of our e-news-
letter, the *BK Communiqué*. Although you're free to unsubscribe, there are
many benefits to sticking around. In every issue of our newsletter you'll find

• A free e-book
• Tips from famous authors
• Discounts on spotlight titles
• Hilarious insider publishing news
• A chance to win a prize for answering a riddle

Best of all, our readers tell us, "Your newsletter is the only one I actually
read." So claim your gift today, and please stay in touch!

Sincerely,

Charlotte Ashlock
Steward of the BK Website

Questions? Comments? Contact me at bkcommunity@bkpub.com.